Black Poets in French

Black
Poets
in French

Edited by

MARIE COLLINS

Rutgers University, Newark

Charles Scribner's Sons · New York

Printed in the United States of America

Library of Congress Catalog Card Number 79-162782

SBN 684-12597-8

ACKNOWLEDGMENTS

The editor is indebted to the following companies for permission to reprint material appearing in this volume:

ATHENEUM PUBLISHERS. For rights to English translation of "Nuit de Sine," "Black Woman," "To the American Negro Soldiers," "Totem," "New York," "Elegy of the Circumcised," reprinted from *Selected Poems* by Léopold Sédar Senghor, translated and introduced by John Reed and Clive Wake, copyright © Oxford University Press 1964. Reprinted by permission of Atheneum Publishers.

GEORGES BORCHARDT, INC. For "Hors des jours étrangers," "Pour saluer le tiers monde," reprinted from *Ferrements* by Aimé Césaire, copyright © 1960, by Éditions du Seuil. For "Barbare," "Mot," reprinted

Acknowledgments

from *Cadastre* by Aimé Césaire, copyright © 1961, by Editions du Seuil. For excerpts from *Un saison au Congo* by Aimé Césaire, copyright © 1939 by Éditions du Seuil. For "Nuit de Sine," "Femme noire," "Aux tirailleurs sénégalais morts pour la France," "Aux soldats négro-américains," "À New York," "Jardin de France," "Totem," "Élégie des circoncis," reprinted from *Poèmes* by Léopold Sédar Senghor, copyright © 1964 by Éditions du Seuil.

ÉDITIONS PIERRE JEAN OSWALD. For excerpts from *Mon pays que voici* by Anthony Phelps, copyright © 1960 by Éditions Pierre Jean Oswald. For excerpts from "Le Contempteur," reprinted from *Epitomé* in the volume *Arc Musical* preceded by *Epitomé* by Tchicaya U 'Tam'si, copyright © Pierre Jean Oswald, publisher, 1970.

ÉDITIONS SEGHERS. For "Litanie d'un sujet française," "Je vous remercie mon Dieu," reprinted from *Légendes et poèmes* by Bernard Dadié, copyright © 1966 by Éditions Seghers. For "Je n'aime pas l'Afrique," reprinted from *Initiation* by Paul Niger, copyright © 1954 by Éditions Seghers. For "Alabama," reprinted from *Journal d'un animal marin* by René Depestre, copyright © 1964 by Éditions Seghers.

GROVE PRESS. For rights to English translation of excerpt from *A Season in the Congo* by Aimé Césaire, translated by Ralph Manheim, copyright © 1968 by Grove Press, Inc.

OXFORD UNIVERSITY PRESS. For rights in Canada for English translation of "Totem," "Nuit de Sine," "Black Woman," "To the American Negro Soldiers," "New York," "Elegy of the Circumcised," reprinted from *Selected Poems* by Léopold Sédar Senghor, translated and introduced by John Reed and Clive Wake, copyright © 1964 by Oxford University Press, London.

PRÉSENCE AFRICAINE. For "Bientôt," "La Complainte du nègre," "Solde," "Obsession," "Trêve," "S.O.S.," "Pour sûr," "Savoir-vivre," "Si souvent," "Ils ont," reprinted from *Pigments* by Léon Damas, copyright © 1962, by *Présence Africaine*. For excerpts from *Cahier d'un retour au pays natal* by Aimé Césaire (bilingual edition), copyright © 1968, by *Présence Africaine*. For excerpts in English reprinted from *Cahier d'un retour au pays natal* by Aimé Césaire, first published by *Présence Africaine*, 1956. This translation published in Penguin Books, 1969, reprinted, 1970; copyright © 1956 by *Présence Africaine*. This translation copyright © 1969 by John Berger and Anna Bostock. For "On les reconnaît," reprinted from *Minerai noir* by René Depestre. Copyright © 1956 by *Présence Africaine*. For "Ode à Patrice

Acknowledgments

Lumumba," "Ode à Malcolm X," reprinted from *Un arc-en-ciel pour l'occident chretien* by René Depestre, copyright © 1967 by *Présence Africaine*. For "Satchmo," reprinted from *Balles d'or* by Guy Tirolien, copyright © 1961 by *Présence Africaine*. For "Vagues," "Afrique," "À une danseuse noire," reprinted from *Coups de pilon* by David Diop, copyright © 1956 by *Présence Africaine*. For "Sur le tombeau de John Kennedy" by Lamine Diakhaté, reprinted from *Nouvelle somme de poésie noire (Présence Africaine, No. 57, 1st quarter 1966)*, copyright © 1966 by *Présence Africaine*. For "Ce que m'a donné la France," "Frère blanc" by Bernard Dadié, reprinted from *Bernard Binlin Dadié*, by C. Quillateau, copyright © 1967 by *Présence Africaine*. For excerpts from *Fusillez-moi* by Édouard Maunick, copyright © 1970 by *Présence Africaine*.

PRESSES UNIVERSITAIRES DE FRANCE. For excerpts from "Bois d'ébène" by Jacques Roumain, and "Me revoici, Harlem" by Jean-F. Brièrre, both reprinted from *L'Anthologie de la nouvelle poésie nègre et malgache* by Léopold Sédar Senghor, copyright © 1948 by Presses Universitaires de France.

THE THIRD PRESS. For rights in the United States and Canada to English translation of "Hors des jours étrangers," "Pour saluer le tiers monde," reprinted from *Ferrements* by Aimé Césaire, copyright © 1960 by Éditions du Seuil. For "Barbare," "Mot," reprinted from *Cadastre* by Aimé Césaire, copyright © 1961 by Éditions du Seuil.

contents

Introduction   xi

part one   **The Caribbean**   1

LÉON DAMAS, POET OF FRENCH GUIANA   3

Bientôt   4
La Complainte du nègre   4
Solde   6
Ils ont   10
Obsession   12
Trêve   12
Si souvent   14
S.O.S.   16
Pour sûr   18
Savoir-vivre   20

MARTINIQUE AND AIMÉ CÉSAIRE   23

Cahier d'un retour au pays natal   24
Une Saison au Congo   36
Hors des jours étrangers   40
Barbare   42
Mot   44
Pour saluer le Tiers Monde   48

Contents

HAITI AND ITS POETS   55

Jacques Roumain
    Bois-d'ébène   56

Jean-F. Brièrre
    Me revoici, Harlem   62

René Depestre
    On les reconnaît   68
    Alabama   68
    Ode à Patrice Lumumba   72
    Ode à Malcolm X   76

Anthony Phelps
    Mon pays que voici   78

TWO POETS FROM GUADELOUPE   87

Paul Niger
    Je n'aime pas l'Afrique   88

Guy Tirolien
    Satchmo   92

part two   **Africa**   101

SENGHOR AND THE POETS OF SENEGAL   103

Léopold Senghor
    Nuit de Sine   104
    Jardin de France   106
    Femme noire   108
    Aux tirailleurs sénégalais morts pour la France   110
    Aux soldats négro-américains   114
    À New York   116
    Élégie des circoncis   122
    Le Totem   126

Contents

David Diop
Vagues 128
Afrique 128
À une danseuse noire 130

Lamine Diakhaté
Sur le tombeau de John Kennedy 132

BERNARD DADIÉ OF THE IVORY COAST 137

Je vous remercie mon Dieu 138
Ce que m'a donné la France 140
Frère blanc 144
Litanie d'un sujet français 146

TCHICAYA U'TAM'SI, POET OF THE CONGO 151

Le Contempteur 152

ÉDOUARD MAUNICK, POET OF MAURITIUS

Fusillez-moi 158

introduction

This collection of poems by passionately committed Blacks who write in French includes poets from the French-speaking territories in the Caribbean and Africa. Part One focuses on the work of writers from the islands of Haiti, Martinique, and Guadeloupe, and the small French department of Guiana on the northeastern tip of the South American mainland. French influence in the Caribbean dates back to the beginning of the seventeenth century, when colonists from France imported large numbers of slaves from Africa to develop prosperous sugar plantations in the territories mentioned. Martinique, Guadeloupe, and French Guiana continued as French colonies until 1946. At that time, they became overseas departments of France in an arrangement that resembles the relationship between Puerto Rico and the United States. The history of Haiti was very different: the Haitians revolted against the French at the time of the French Revolution, and by 1804 the French forces and all white settlers had been expelled. Since then, Haiti has been independent. French and Creole remain as the only significant languages spoken and written in these territories.

Part II of the book is devoted to French-speaking poets from Africa, where French exploration began in the sixteenth century. By the outbreak of World War I, France, in competition with other European imperialist powers, had established colonies in three major areas south of the Sahara in Black Africa: Equatorial Africa, including Cameroon; the countries of the "Entente Sahil-

Benin" — Ivory Coast, Dahomey, Togo, Niger, and Upper Volta; and the neighboring countries of the Senegal River basin — Mauritania, Mali, Senegal, and Guinea; as well as on the island of Madagascar in the Indian Ocean.

In the wake of the Algerian crisis that brought an end to the Fourth French Republic in 1958 and returned DeGaulle to power as president of the new Fifth Republic, the sub-Saharan territories, with the exception of Guinea, voted to remain tied to France as members of the Communauté Française (the French Community). This union lasted only 18 months. By 1960 the rapidly evolving process of decolonization had ended in total independence for all the territories.

Colonialism left a difficult legacy to the newly independent countries of Africa. Like other colonial powers, France had destroyed the structure of native society in its African territories and imposed French ideas, traditions, and ways of thinking, a situation that is reflected in many of these poems. It had also left the French language, which continues in the courts and government offices as the official language of all the former French colonies. French also serves as the language of the educated classes, the newspapers, and written literature — although oral literature continues to be composed, as it has been for centuries, in many tribal languages.

By 1930 the growing Black middle classes, concentrated in the urbanized areas of French-speaking Africa and the Caribbean, had begun to educate their sons in Paris. An intellectual Black elite came to be centered around the University and the Grandes Écoles, the prestigious institutes of higher education whose graduates were assured important administrative and teaching jobs. Influenced and inspired by Claude MacKay, Jean Toomer, Langston Hughes, Countee Cullen, and other writers of the American Negro Renaissance of the 1920s, the idealistic young Black students gathered in the French capital joined forces, tried to forget their differences as West Indians and Africans, and stressed their unity as Blacks, celebrating their pride in their race and revolting against white domination and exploitation. The result of their efforts was the Negritude movement. This movement, which marks the flowering of Black consciousness in the French language, encompassed some of the very greatest Black writers and affected all who followed, including poets at work today.

The movement crystalized in 1932, when a group of students from Martinique led by Étienne Lero published a manifesto entitled "Legitimate Defense." In this statement they denounced the tendency of Black Caribbean writers to forego their Blackness in an endeavor to make their works indistinguishable from those of white writers in French. This revolt and call to arms deeply touched the three future masters of the Negritude movement, Léon-Gontran Damas of Guiana, Aimé Césaire of Martinique, and Léopold Sédar Senghor of Senegal, all of who were pursuing university degrees in Paris at that time.

In praising Blackness, the manifesto used many arguments that had been developed by the Communists and Surrealists. Surrealism, a French literary movement of the 1920s, proclaimed the triumph of irrationality in man and called for total liberation in literature from traditional forms. Its insistence upon scandalizing the bourgeoisie and provoking a social revolution, its anti-rationalism, and its celebration of the art of "primitive" peoples were especially attractive to the young Black students in Paris, whose race had been considered inferior for the very reason that its culture was not "rational." Freud's investigations of the importance of the unconscious had questioned the entire rational structure of the Western tradition. Drawing on this, the Surrealists considered the poet as a visionary or "seer" and revered the power of the "word" in a way that echoed the oral tradition of African poetry. The West Indian intellectuals used the tenets of Surrealism in their campaign to dismantle the structures of the white race that had enslaved and victimized them.

Introduction

The "Legitimate Defense" manifesto catalyzed the Black students in Paris. Under the leadership of Césaire, Damas, and Senghor, in 1934 they launched the new magazine *The Black Student*. The review published just one issue, but its impact was lasting. Its aim had been cultural, and the entire Black race was included in its perspectives — Africans as well as West Indians. *The Black Student* haughtily affirmed the rights of the Black race in its revolt against racism and the imperialism of the West. It was a call for total liberation in the reconquered pride of the Black man and an awareness of the historical values of his race.

After the demise of *The Black Student,* Césaire continued the fight against cultural assimilation, while Senghor sought to analyze and exalt the traditional values of Black Africa. Together with Damas, they plunged into the writings of anthropologists such as Froebenius and Delafosse who described the splendors of African civilizations of the past. What Césaire discovered in those books awakened him. He saw that the white colonial education of which he was such a dazzling product, and which stressed the superiority of French culture and the inferiority of the Black race, was based on exploitation and a deliberate misreading of history for domination. Like Damas, Césaire had been raised in a white world, 3,000 miles distant and three centuries away from the land and heritage of Africa. In that world the French colonial policy of assimilation thrust Blackness into an atmosphere of shame. Césaire's encounter with the brilliant young Senghor, who had enjoyed the privilege of an African childhood in his native Senegal, was crucial. Senghor's serene harmony with his ancestral heritage heightened the Martinican's resentment that he himself had been kept ignorant of the culturally rich past of his African forebears.

Césaire, Senghor, and Damas, the three "founders" of Negritude, all firmly rejected the assimilation that imposed French culture and excluded traditional Black values. Negritude was born in the ferment of this rejection, and the first creative works springing from the three founders' passionate convictions soon appeared. In 1937 Damas published *Pigments,* an astonishing collection of tense, spare, violent poems in which the theme of repudiation of assimilation dominates. The poems strive to make the Black reader share the poet's rejection of the disintegrating Western civilization that had crushed the Black man. Damas, influenced by Mallarmé and the Surrealists, forged in his book a poetic language of jagged rhythms and colloquial speech that was lifted from banality by its immediacy and commitment.

Aimé Césaire's long poem *Cahier d'un retour au pays natal (Return to My Native Land),* written in 1938 and published in 1939, was an effort by the poet to fuse his personal experience with that of his race. Like the French poet-seer Arthur Rimbaud (1854–1891), Césaire deliberately displaced syntax and sculpted the French language to fit his own needs, using rare words and often private symbols drawn from his island home. This aggressive epic poem is still his most widely read work.

Senghor began to write poetry in 1936, though his first collection, *Chants d'ombre (Shadow Songs),* was not published until after the war in 1945. Securely anchored in the African society of his birth, Senghor was able in his poems to mine the sources of Black experience, just as the movement demanded. The sonorous, long verse lines of Senghor's work reflect the oral tradition of African verse that exists in many tribal languages and is meant to be sung. Senghor celebrates the moral values of a pastoral and warrior society, the continuing presence of ancestors, and the profound African reverence for life, love, and festivities. The suffering of the Black race is not absent, for Senghor too had experienced at first hand in Europe the bite of white racism. Yet he disdains hatred, underlining instead the capacity of the Black race to love.

With the advent of World War II, Césaire returned with his wife Suzanne to Martinique to teach and to found the review *Tropiques.* Senghor was captured by the Germans while serving in the French army, but upon his release in 1941 he returned to Paris, where he and Alioune Diop, a fellow Senegalese, formed a group that eventually produced the monthly *Présence Africaine* in 1947. This cultural review of the Black world remains to this day the most respected periodical of African affairs. Currently it appears in two editions: French and English.

In 1948 Senghor published the now legendary *Anthologie de la nouvelle poésie nègre et malgache (Anthology of the New Black and Malagasy Poetry in French)*. A scorching introduction by Jean-Paul Sartre, "Black Orpheus," which applauded the poets of Negritude and indicted the white colonial world, helped to launch the volume. The French-speaking world awoke to the wealth of talent and the authenticity of the claims of these extraordinary spokesmen for a long-oppressed race.

Senghor's anthololgy presented his own poems and those of Césaire and Damas, as well as poems by other African, West Indian, and Malagasy poets (from Madagascar). It also included three Haitian poets of the Indigenist movement, Roumain, Brièrre, and Bellance. These men were truly the predecessors of Negritude. Haitian literature, which had flourished since the country won its independence in the early nineteenth century, had been given a new direction in the 1920s by Jean Price Mars and Jacques Roumain. At their urging, Haitian writers began to cast off the influence of France and attempted to Haitianize the literature of their country. No longer interested in imitating white models, they began to investigate their African heritage, particularly the local customs and beliefs that stemmed from it; and they discovered the great riches of Haitian folklore and traditions. This renaissance in Haiti preceded the birth of the Negritude movement in Paris by at least 10 years.

The poets of Senghor's anthology included here, besides those mentioned above, are Paul Niger and Guy Tirolien from Guadeloupe, David Diop from Senegal, and Bernard Dadié from the Ivory Coast. Space, unfortunately, does not permit the inclusion

of the famous "three R's" from Madagascar, Ranaivo, Rabe-
mananjara, and Rabéarivelo, nor Birago Diop from Senegal, nor
countless others from the vast and various French-speaking
Black domains in Africa and the West Indies.

Senghor's anthology inspired many young Black poets writing
in French. Several of these literary heirs are included in this
book: the Haitians René Depestre and Anthony Phelps, the
Senegalese Lamine Diakhaté, the Congolese Tchicaya U'Tam'si,
and the Mauritian Édouard Maunick. Each continues and ampli-
fies the basic themes and approaches of the original poets of the
Negritude movement: powerful pride in Blackness; sorrowful
and bitter evocations of the horrendous history of slavery; sear-
ingly eloquent anti-colonialism; repudiation of assimilated
white culture; the warmth, color, and beauty of the African
respect for life; and emphasis on the overwhelming capacity of
the proud Black race to love, despite its suffering. These are the
obsessions of Black writers all over the world, heirs of the great
tribes of the African continent, wherever they may have been
scattered in the Black Diaspora by the ignominious slave trade.

Negritude was essentially a revolt against the oppression of
the Black race by the white race, fused with the desire to restore
human dignity to the Black man who had borne four centuries of
servitude. The word was coined by Césaire in *Cahier d'un retour
au pays natal*. He later defined it as "the simple recognition of
the fact of being black, the acceptance of this fact, of our black
destiny, history and culture." The movement's cry of rage was
expressed in French because that language could reach the op-
pressor, although it is not the native language of most Black
peoples. More than 400 different tribal languages are spoken in
Africa, for example. For the time being at least, French and
English are a unifying means of communication within that con-
tinent and abroad. However, Africa has had a rich native litera-
ture in tribal languages for centuries, handed down orally by
"griots," official poets, or minstrels. Linguists are currently re-

cording this oral literature in many African languages and working out alphabets for those many languages that never had a system of writing. The novelists and poets of Africa have been transcribing the legends, tales, and lyric and epic poems of their native tribes for years. Senghor has translated into French the poetry of the Wolof (the dominant tribe in Senegal), and U'Tam'si and Dadié have also collected and translated local legends and tales. In the Caribbean, most of the islanders communicate in Creole, a language derived from French and various African tongues. In Haiti, especially, there is a body of literature in Creole, which is no longer considered merely a dialect of untutored French, but a full-fledged language in its own right.

Many writers in the French-speaking countries of Africa and the Caribbean will continue to use French, since they are eager to reach a wider public. But each poet brings to French startling new possibilities that spring from his profoundly Black African soul. In the mastery and reshaping of the language to the rhythms and needs of their passionate commitment, the poets of Negritude, as this sampling hopes to illustrate, display an infinite variety.

The poems chosen for this anthology were selected for their beauty, their importance in the movement, and their appeal to American students. My deepest apologies for the exclusion of so many. And my great thanks to Ann McAdams, Yanick deVastey, Vincent Guilloton, and the sisters and brothers of Rutgers-Newark who inspired this volume.

M.C.

Black Poets in French

part one

The Caribbean

This section presents works by poets from Haiti, Martinique, Guadeloupe, and French Guiana. Haiti's century and a half of independence and its strong literary tradition account for the large number of Haitian poets included here. In the nineteenth century Haiti's many writers produced works that were usually derivative of literary currents in mainland France; nevertheless these men opened the way for the more nationalistic writers of the twentieth century. In the 1920s the Indigenist movement celebrated the African heritage of the Haitian population. Precursors of the founders of Negritude, the Indigenists found no echo elsewhere in the Caribbean except in the Martinican novelist René Maran, whose *Batouala* won the Prix Goncourt in 1921. This book, reflecting Maran's experience as a colonial administrator in French West Africa, was the first accurate presentation of French colonial policy from the Black man's point of view.

Two poets of the Negritude movement, Léon Damas of Guiana and Aimé Césaire of Martinique, open this section. They express the alienation of the Black man ripped by the colonial system from his ancestral Africa and its traditions, and they picture the Caribbean as the home of millions of descendents of the Black Diaspora. The section ends with four poets from Haiti and two from Guadeloupe.

1

Léon Damas

LÉON DAMAS, POET OF FRENCH GUIANA

French Guiana, birthplace of Léon-Gontran Damas, is ironically best known for its penal colony, Devil's Island. Born in 1912 into a middle-class mulatto family, Damas was brought up by his mother to observe the strictest code of white French bourgeois manners. His sardonic attitude toward this education for assimilation is painfully evident in his poems. After secondary studies in Martinique, where he met Aimé Césaire, Damas was sent to Paris to study law. There he met Césaire again, as well as Senghor, and writers of the *Black Student* and American Negro Renaissance groups, Countee Cullen, Jean Toomer, Langston Hughes. When his political activities prompted his parents to cut off his funds, Damas lived hand to mouth as a Black in a white culture, performing menial tasks, an experience that sharpened his already acute sense of outrage. Fortunately his fellow Black students rescued him for writing by securing a scholarship from the French government.

The following poems are all from Damas' first collection, *Pigments*, published in 1937. It was the first literary expression of Negritude and gave a dazzling modern form to the themes of the movement, particularly the revolt against white domination and the repudiation of assimilated white culture. The ferocity of the themes is deftly expressed in dry staccato rhythms echoing the jazz cadences so popular at the time. Damas has continued to write poetry and prose, while performing cultural missions for UNESCO after a brief term as a deputy.

BIENTÔT

Bientôt
je n'aurai pas que dansé
bientôt
je n'aurai pas que chanté
bientôt
je n'aurai pas que frotté
bientôt
je n'aurai pas que trempé
bientôt
je n'aurai pas que dansé
chanté
frotté
trempé
frotté
chanté
dansé
        Bientôt

LA COMPLAINTE DU NÈGRE

Pour Robert Goffin

Ils me l'ont rendue
la vie
plus lourde et lasse

Mes aujourd'hui ont chacun sur mon jadis
de gros yeux qui roulent de rancoeur
de honte

SOON

Soon
I won't only have danced
soon
I won't only have sung
soon
I won't only have scrubbed
soon
I won't only have soaked
soon
I won't only have danced
sung
scrubbed
soaked
scrubbed
sung
danced
　　　Soon

THE NEGRO'S BALLAD

For Robert Goffin

They've given it back to me
life
heavier and more weary

My todays on my yesterdays fix
huge eyes rolling with rancor
with shame

Léon Damas

Les jours inexorablement
tristes
jamais n'ont cessé d'être
à la mémoire
de ce que fut
ma vie tronquée

Va encore
mon hébétude
du temps jadis
de coups de corde noueux
de corps calcinés
de l'orteil au dos calcinés
de chair morte
de tisons
de fer rouge
de bras brisés
sous le fouet qui se déchaîne
sous le fouet qui fait marcher la plantation
et s'abreuver de sang de mon sang de sang la sucrerie
et la bouffarde du commandeur crâner au ciel.

SOLDE

Pour Aimé Césaire

J'ai l'impression d'être ridicule
dans leurs souliers
dans leur smoking
dans leur plastron
dans leur faux-col
dans leur monocle
dans leur melon

The days inexorably
sad
have never ceased to be
in memory
of what was
my mutilated life

Still lasts my daze
from the past
of lashes from knotted cords
of charred bodies
of the toe in charred backs
of dead flesh
of red hot branding irons
of broken arms
under the unleashed whip
under the whip that works the plantation
and quenches with blood my blood of bloods the sugar mill
and the lash of the foreman swaggering against the sky.

CLEARANCE

For Aimé Césaire

I've the feeling I'm ridiculous
in their dancing slippers
in their tuxedo
in their starched shirt-front
in their stiff collar
in their monocle
in their derby

Léon Damas

J'ai l'impression d'être ridicule
avec mes orteils qui ne sont pas faits
pour transpirer du matin jusqu'au soir qui déshabille
avec l'emmaillotage qui m'affaiblit les membres
et enlève à mon corps sa beauté de cache-sexe

J'ai l'impression d'être ridicule
avec mon cou en cheminée d'usine
avec ces maux de tête qui cessent
chaque fois que je salue quelqu'un

J'ai l'impression d'être ridicule
dans leurs salons
dans leurs manières
dans leurs courbettes
dans leur multiple besoin de singeries

J'ai l'impression d'être ridicule
avec tout ce qu'ils racontent
jusqu'à ce qu'ils vous servent l'après-midi
un peu d'eau chaude
et des gâteaux enrhumés

J'ai l'impression d'être ridicule
avec les théories qu'ils assaisonnent
au goût de leurs besoins
de leurs passions
de leurs instincts ouverts la nuit
en forme de paillasson

J'ai l'impression d'être ridicule
parmi eux complice
parmi eux souteneur
parmi eux égorgeur

I've the feeling I'm ridiculous
with my toes not made
to perspire from morning till evening undresses
with the swaddling clothes that weaken my members
and rob my body of its loin-cloth beauty

I've the feeling I'm ridiculous
with my neck stiff as a factory smokestack
with these headaches that stop
each time I nod to someone

I've the feeling I'm ridiculous
in their drawing rooms
in their manners
in their little bows
in their multiple need for aping

I've the feeling I'm ridiculous
with all the tales they tell
until they serve you in the afternoon
a little hot water
and some sickly cakes

I've the feeling I'm ridiculous
with the theories they season
to the taste of their needs
of their passions
of their instincts open at night
in the shape of a door mat

I've the feeling I'm ridiculous
among them accomplice
among them pimp
among them throat-slitter

Léon Damas

les mains effroyablement rouges
du sang de leur ci-vi-li-sa-tion

ILS ONT

Ils ont si bien su faire
si bien su faire les choses
les choses
qu'un jour nous avons tout
nous avons tout foutu de nous-mêmes
tout foutu de nous-mêmes en l'air

Qu'ils aient si bien su faire
si bien su faire les choses
les choses
qu'un jour nous ayons tout foutu
nous ayons tout foutu de nous-mêmes
tout foutu de nous-mêmes en l'air

Il ne faudrait pourtant pas grand'chose
pourtant pas grand'chose
grand'chose
pour qu'en un jour enfin tout aille
tout aille
aille
dans le sens de notre race à nous
de notre race à nous

Il ne faudrait pourtant pas grand'chose
pourtant pas grand'chose
pas grand'chose
pas grand'chose

my hands horribly red
with the blood of their ci-vi-li-za-tion

THEY HAVE

They knew so well how to operate
so well how to do things
things
that one day we blew it
we blew it all by ourselves
completely blew it

Since they knew so well how to operate
so well how to do things
things
one day we blew it
we blew it all by ourselves
completely blew it

It wouldn't really take very much
not really very much
very much
for it all to finally in one day go
all go
go
in the direction of our own race
of our own race

It really wouldn't take very much
not really very much
not very much
not very much

OBSESSION

Un goût de sang me vient
un goût de sang me monte
m'irrite le nez
la gorge
les yeux

Un goût de sang me vient
un goût de sang m'emplit
le nez
la gorge
les yeux

Un goût de sang me vient
âcrement vertical
pareil
à l'obsession païenne
des encensoirs

TRÊVE

Trêve de blues
de martèlements de piano
de trompette bouchée
de folie claquant des pieds
à la satisfaction du rythme

Trêve de séances à tant le swing
autour de rings
qu'énervent
des cris de fauves

OBSESSION

A taste of blood comes to me
a taste of blood rises up in me
irritates my nose
my throat
my eyes

A taste of blood comes to me
a taste of blood fills
my nose
my throat
my eyes

a taste of blood
bitterly vertical
similar
to the pagan obsession
for censers

TRUCE

Truce from the blues
from hammering pianos
from muted trumpets
from madness stamping its feet
to the rhythm's satisfaction

Truce from countless sessions of swing
around the ring
tense
from savage roars

Trêve de lâchage
de léchage
de lèche
et
d'une attitude
d'hyperassimilés

Trêve un instant
d'une vie de bon enfant
et de désirs
et de besoins
et d'égoïsmes
particuliers.

SI SOUVENT

Si souvent mon sentiment de race m'effraie
autant qu'un chien aboyant la nuit
une mort prochaine
quelconque
je me sens prêt à écumer toujours de rage
contre ce qui m'entoure
contre ce qui m'empêche
à jamais d'être
un homme

Et rien
rien ne saurait autant calmer ma haine
qu'une belle mare
de sang
faite
de ces coutelas tranchants
qui mettent à nu
les mornes à rhum

Léon Damas

Truce from letting up
from lapping up
from licking up
and from an attitude
of the super-assimilated[1]

Truce for an instant
from the careless life
and from private
desires
and needs
and selfishness

SO OFTEN

So often my feeling of race frightens me
Like a dog barking in the night
at some kind of
nearby death
I always feel ready to foam with rage
against what surrounds me
against what prevents me
from ever being
a man

And nothing
nothing could calm my hatred so much
as a beautiful pool
of blood
made
with the sharpened cutlasses
that strip bare
the hills of rum

[1]The Black man who adopts white manners and attitudes.

S.O.S.

A ce moment-là seul
comprendrez-vous donc tous
quand leur viendra l'idée
bientôt cette idée leur viendra
de vouloir vous en bouffer du nègre
à la manière d'Hitler
bouffant du juif
sept jours fascistes
sur
sept

A ce moment-là seul
comprendrez-vous donc tous
quand leur supériorité
s'étalera
d'un bout à l'autre de leurs boulevards
et qu'alors
vous les verrez
vraiment tout se permettre
ne plus se contenter de rire avec l'index inquiet
de voir passer un nègre
mais
froidement matraquer
mais
froidement descendre
mais
froidement étendre
mais froidement

Léon Damas

S.O.S.

Only then
will you all understand
when they get the idea
soon they'll get that idea
to want to gobble up the Negro
like Hitler
gobbling up the Jew
seven fascist days
out of seven

Only then
will you all understand
when their superiority
spreads
from one end to another of their streets
and then
you'll see them
really allowing themselves everything
no longer content to laugh behind a worried finger
at seeing a Negro pass
but
coldly clubbing
but
coldly knocking down
but
coldly stretching out
but coldly

matraquer
descendre
étendre
et
couper leur sexe aux nègres
pour en faire des bougies pour leurs églises

POUR SÛR

Pour sûr j'en aurai
marre
sans même attendre
qu'elles prennent
les choses
l'allure
d'un camembert bien fait

Alors
je vous mettrai les pieds dans le plat
ou bien tout simplement
la main au collet
de tout ce qui m'emmerde en gros caractères
colonisation
civilisation
assimilation
et la suite

En attendant
vous m'entendrez souvent
claquer la porte

clubbing
knocking down
stretching out
and
cutting off the Negroes' sex
to make candles for their churches

FOR SURE

For sure I'll get
sick of it
without even waiting
for things
to take on
the look
of a ripe camembert

Then
I'll stick your nose in it
or more simply
grab by the collar
everything I crap on in capital letters
colonization
civilization
assimilation
and the rest

Meanwhile
you'll often hear me
slam the door

SAVOIR-VIVRE

Pour Étienne Zabulon

On ne bâille pas chez moi
comme ils bâillent chez eux
avec
la main sur la bouche

Je veux bâiller sans tralalas
le corps recroquevillé
dans les parfums qui tourmentent la vie
que je me suis faite
de leur museau de chien d'hiver
de leur soleil qui ne pourrait
pas même
tiédir
l'eau de coco qui faisait glouglou
dans mon ventre au réveil

Laissez-moi bâiller
la main
là
sur le coeur
à l'obsession de tout ce à quoi
j'ai en un jour un seul
tourné le dos

Léon Damas

SOCIAL GRACES

For Étienne Zabulon

They don't yawn at home
the way they yawn here
with
their hand over their mouth

I want to yawn without airs
my body hunched
into the perfumes that torment the life
I've made for myself
from their dog-faced winter
from their sun that couldn't
even
warm
the coconut milk that would gurgle
in my belly when I'd wake up

Let me yawn,
my hand
there
on my heart,
at the obsession with everything that
in one single day I
turned my back on

Aimé Césaire

MARTINIQUE AND AIMÉ CÉSAIRE

Martinique, a volcanic island now an overseas department of France, was the birthplace of Aimé Césaire in 1913. The majority of the island's largely peasant population are Black descendants of slaves imported to work the colony's plantations. Césaire, born into a family of limited means, could not fail to respond as a child to the poverty, resignation, and despair of the people, and his poetry is marked by outrage at the imbalance between rich and poor, as well as revolt against the inferiority complex left by colonial rule. Studying in Paris at the time of the "Legitimate Defense" and *Black Student* groups, he coined the word "negritude" which came to name the literary movement. His long poem "Return to My Native Land" is a blistering cry of pain, outrage, scandal, and revolt that calls on Blacks to take pride in their race and to reject assimilation to white culture. Published in 1939, it is still his most read poem, despite its length of 70 pages. Césaire's later poetry is often inaccessible and surrealistically obscure. While writing in many genres, the poet represents Martinique in the French Assembly and serves as mayor of the island's capital, Fort-de-France.

Aimé Césaire

CAHIER D'UN RETOUR AU PAYS NATAL (fragments)

Ce qui est à moi, ces quelques milliers de mortiférés qui tournent en rond dans la calebasse d'un île et ce qui est à moi aussi, l'archipel arqué comme le désir inquiet de se nier, on dirait une anxiété maternelle pour protéger la ténuité plus délicate qui sépare l'une de l'autre Amérique; et ses flancs qui secrètent pour l'Europe la bonne liqueur d'un Gulf Stream, et l'un des deux versants d'incandescence entre quoi l'Equateur funambule vers l'Afrique. Et mon île non-clôture, sa claire audace debout à l'arrière de cette polynésie, devant elle, la Guadeloupe fendue en deux de sa raie dorsale et de même misère que nous, Haïti où la négritude se mit debout pour la première fois et dit qu'elle croyait à son humanité et la comique petite queue de la Floride où d'un nègre s'achève la strangulation, et l'Afrique gigantesquement chenillant jusqu'au pied hispanique de l'Europe, sa nudité où la Mort fauche à larges andains.

Et je me dis Bordeaux et Nantes et Liverpool et New-York et
    San-Francisco
pas un bout de ce monde qui ne porte mon empreinte digitale
et mon calcanéum sur le dos des gratte-ciel et ma crasse
dans le scintillement des gemmes!
Qui peut se vanter d'avoir mieux que moi?
Virginie. Tennessee. Géorgie. Alabama.
Putréfactions monstrueuses de révoltes
inopérantes,
marais de sang putrides
trompettes absurdement bouchées
Terres rouges, terres sanguines, terres consanguines.

Ce qui est à moi aussi: une petite
cellule dans le Jura,

Aimé Césaire

RETURN TO MY NATIVE LAND (excerpts)

These are mine: these few gangrenous thousands who rattle in this calabash of an island. And this too is mine: this archipelago arched with anxiety as though to deny itself, as though she were a mother anxious to protect the tenuous delicacy with which her two Americas are joined; this archipelago whose flanks secrete for Europe the sweet liquid of the Gulf Stream; this archipelago which is one side of the shining passage through which the Equator walks its tightrope to Africa. My island, my non-enclosure, whose bright courage stands at the back of my polynesia; in front, Guadeloupe split in two by its dorsal ridge and as wretched as we ourselves; Haiti where negritude rose to its feet for the first time and said it believed in its own humanity; and the comic little tail of Florida where they are just finishing strangling a Negro; and Africa gigantically caterpillaring as far as the Spanish foot of Europe: the nakedness of Africa where the scythe of Death swings wide.

My name is Bordeaux and Nantes and Liverpool and New York
    and San Francisco
not a corner of this world but carries my thumb-print
and my heel-mark on the backs of skyscrapers and my dirt
in the glitter of jewels!
Who can boast of more than I?
Virginia. Tennessee. Georgia. Alabama.
Monstrous putrefactions of revolts
coming to nothing,
putrid marshes of blood
trumpets ridiculously blocked
Red earth, blood earth, blood brother earth.

Mine too a small
cell in the Jura,

une petite cellule, la neige la double de barreaux blancs
la neige est un geôlier blanc qui monte
la garde devant une prison

Ce qui est à moi
c'est un homme seul emprisonné de
blanc
c'est un homme seul qui défie les cris
blancs de la mort blanche
(TOUSSAINT, TOUSSAINT
LOUVERTURE)
c'est un homme qui fascine l'épervier blanc de la mort blanche
c'est un homme seul dans la mer inféconde de sable blanc
c'est un moricaud vieux dressé contre les eaux du ciel
La mort décrit un cercle brillant au-dessus de cet homme
la mort étoile doucement au-dessus de sa tête
la mort souffle, folle, dans la cannaie mûre de ses bras
la mort galope dans la prison comme un cheval blanc
la mort luit dans l'ombre comme des yeux de chat
la mort hoquète comme l'eau sous les Cayes
la mort est un oiseau blessé
la mort décroît
la mort vacille
la mort est un patyura ombrageux
la mort expire dans une blanche mare
de silence.

· · · · ·

ô lumière amicale
ô fraîche source de la lumière
ceux qui n'ont inventé ni la poudre ni la boussole
ceux qui n'ont jamais su dompter la vapeur ni l'électricité

the snow strengthens the small cell with white bars
the snow is a white
gaoler who stands guard in front of a prison

This man is mine
a man alone, imprisoned by
whiteness
a man alone defying the white
cries of a white death
(TOUSSAINT, TOUSSAINT
LOUVERTURE)[1]
a man who fascinates the white sparrow-hawk of white death
a man alone in the sterile sea of white sand
an old nigger standing upright against the waters of the sky
Death describes a shining circle above this man
death is a gentle star above his head
death, driven mad, blowing in the ripe cane plantation of his
　　arms
death galloping through the prison like a white horse
death gleaming like a cat's eyes in the dark
death hiccuping like water underneath the Reefs
death is a wounded bird
death wanes
death vacillates
death is a shadowy pasture
death expires in a white pool
of silence.

· · · · ·

o well-disposed light
o fresh source of light
those who invented neither gunpowder nor compass
those who tamed neither steam nor electricity

[1]Haitian slave who led his people in their successful revolt against French
colonial rule.

27

Aimé Césaire

ceux qui n'ont exploré ni les mers ni le ciel
mais ceux sans qui la terre ne serait pas la terre
gibbosité d'autant plus bienfaisante que la terre déserte
davantage la terre
silo où se préserve et mûrit ce que la terre a de plus terre
ma négritude n'est pas une pierre, sa surdité ruée contre la
    clameur du jour
ma négritude n'est pas une taie d'eau morte sur l'oeil mort de
    la terre
ma négritude n'est ni une tour ni une cathédrale

elle plonge dans la chair rouge du sol
elle plonge dans la chair ardente du ciel
elle troue l'accablement opaque de sa droite patience.

Eia pour le Kaïlcédrat royal!
Eia pour ceux qui n'ont jamais rien inventé
pour ceux qui n'ont jamais rien exploré
pour ceux qui n'ont jamais rien dompté

mais ils s'abandonnent, saisis, à l'essence de toute chose
ignorants des surfaces mais saisis par le mouvement de toute
    chose
insoucieux de dompter, mais jouant le jeu du monde

véritablement les fils aînés du monde
poreux à tous les souffles du monde
aire fraternelle de tous les souffles du monde
lit sans drain de toutes les eaux du monde
étincelle du feu sacré du monde

those who explored neither sea nor sky
but without whom the earth would not be the earth
We the hump growing more benign
as more and more the earth abandons its own
we the silo
storing to ripen
all of the earth that belongs most to the earth
my negritude is not a stone,
nor deafness flung out against the clamour of the day
my negritude is not a white speck of dead water
on the dead eye of the earth
my negritude is neither tower nor cathedral

it plunges into the red flesh of the soil
it plunges into the blazing flesh of the sky
my negritude riddles with holes
the dense affliction of its worthy patience.

Heia for the royal Kailcedrate![1]
Heia for those who have never invented anything
those who never explored anything
those who never tamed anything

those who give themselves up to the essence of all things
ignorant of surfaces but struck by the movement of all things
free of the desire to tame but familiar with the play of the world

truly the eldest sons of the world
open to all the breaths of the world
fraternal territory of all breaths
undrained bed of the waters of the world
spark of the sacred fire of the world

[1] A shady tree indigenous to Senegal.

chair de la chair du monde palpitant du mouvement même du
    monde!
Tiède petit matin de vertus ancestrales

Sang! Sang! tout notre sang ému par le coeur mâle du soleil
ceux qui savent la féminité de la lune au corps d'huile
l'exaltation réconciliée de l'antilope et de l'étoile
ceux dont la survie chemine en la germination de l'herbe!
Eia parfait cercle du monde et close concordance!

Ecoutez le monde blanc
horriblement las de son effort immense
ses articulations rebelles craquer sous les étoiles dures
ses raideurs d'acier bleu transperçant la chair mystique
écoute ses victoires proditoires trompeter ses défaites
écoute aux alibis grandioses son piètre trébuchement

Pitié pour nos vainqueurs omniscients et naïfs!

. . . . .

donnez-moi la foi sauvage du sorcier
donnez à mes mains puissance de modeler
donnez à mon âme la trempe de l'épée
je ne me dérobe point. Faites de ma tête une tête de proue
et de moi-même, mon coeur, ne faites ni un père, ni un frère,
ni un fils, mais le père, mais le frère, mais le fils,
ni un mari, mais l'amant de cet unique peuple.

Faites-moi rebelle à toute vanité, mais docile à son génie
comme le poing à l'allongée du bras!

flesh of the flesh of the world pumping with the very movement
    of the world
Warm small hours of ancestral virtues

Blood! Blood! all our blood roused by the male heart of the sun
those who know the femininity of the moon with her body of oil
the rapture of reconciliation between antelope and star
those who continue to live in the germination of grass!
Heia perfect circle of the world and the fitness of agreement!

Listen to the white world
appallingly weary from its immense effort
the crack of its joints rebelling under the hardness of the stars
its stiff blue steel piercing the mystic flesh
listen to the proclaimed victories which trumpet their defeats
listen to their grandiose alibis (stumbling so lamely)

Pity for our conquerors, all-knowing and naïve!

. . . . .

Give me the sorcerer's savage faith
give my hands the power to mould
give my soul the temper of the sword
I will stand firm. Make of my head a prow
and of myself make neither a father
nor a brother nor a son
but the father, the brother, the son
do not make me a husband, but the lover of this unique people

Make me rebellious against all vanity but docile to its genius
like the fist of our extended arm

Aimé Césaire

Faites-moi commissaire de son sang
faites-moi dépositaire de son ressentiment
faites de moi un homme de terminaison
faites de moi un homme d'initiation
faite de moi un homme de recueillement
mais faites aussi de moi un homme d'ensemencement

faites de moi l'exécuteur de ces oeuvres hautes
voici le temps de se ceindre les reins comme un vaillant homme–

Mais les faisant, mon coeur, préservez-moi de toute haine
ne faites point de moi cet homme de haine pour qui je n'ai que
        haine
car pour me cantonner en cette unique race
vous savez pourtant mon amour tyrannique
vous savez que ce n'est point par haine des autres races
que je m'exige bêcheur de cette unique race
que ce que je veux
c'est pour la faim universelle
pour la soif universelle

la sommer libre enfin
de produire de son intimité close
la succulence des fruits.

                              .   .   .   .   .

Et voici soudain que force et vie m'assaillent comme un taureau
et l'onde de vie circonvient la papille du morne, et voilà toutes
les veines et veinules qui s'affairent au sang neuf et l'énorme
poumon des cyclones qui respire et le feu thésaurisé des volcans
et le gigantesque pouls sismique qui bat maintenant la mesure
d'un corps vivant en mon ferme embrasement.

Make me the steward of its blood
make me the trustee of its rancour
make me a man of ending
make me a man of beginning
make me a man of harvesting
but also make me a man of sowing

make of me its executioner
the time has come to gird my loins like a man of courage

but at the execution let my heart preserve me from all hate
do not make of me that man of hate for whom I have only hate
I was born of this unique race
yet knowing my tyrannical love you know
it is not by hatred of other races that I prosecute for mine.
All that I would wish is
to answer the universal hunger
the universal thirst

to prescribe at last this unique race free
to produce from its tight intimacies the succulence of fruit.

· · · · ·

And now suddenly strength and life attack me like a bull the
wave of life streams over the nipple of the Morne,[1] veins and
veinlets throng with new blood, the enormous lung of cyclones
breathing, the fire hoarded in volcanoes, and the gigantic seis-
mic pulse beats the measure of a living body within my blaze.

[1]Small hill.

Aimé Césaire

Et nous sommes debout maintenant, mon pays et moi, les cheveux dans le vent, ma main petite maintenant dans son poing énorme et la force n'est pas en nous, mais au-dessus de nous, dans une voix qui vrille la nuit et l'audience comme la pénétrance d'une guêpe apocalyptique. Et la voix prononce que l'Europe nous a pendant des siècles gavés de mensonges et gonflés de pestilences,

car il n'est point vrai que l'oeuvre de l'homme est finie
que nous n'avons rien à faire au monde
que nous parasitons le monde
qu'il suffit que nous nous mettions au pas du monde
mais l'oeuvre de l'homme vient seulement de commencer
et il reste à l'homme à conquérir toute interdiction immobilisée
    aux coins de sa ferveur
et aucune race ne possède le monopole de la beauté, de l'intelligence, de la force
    ligence, de la force
et il est place pour tous au rendez-vous de la conquête et nous savons maintenant que le soleil tourne autour de notre terre éclairant la parcelle qu'a fixée notre volonté seule et que toute étoile chute de ciel en terre à notre commandement sans limite.

Upright now, my country and I, hair in the wind, my hand small in its enormous fist and our strength not inside us but above in a voice that bores through the night and its listeners like the sting of an apocalyptic wasp. And the voice declares that for centuries Europe has stuffed us with lies and crammed us with plague,

for it is not true that:
the work of man is finished
we have nothing to do in the world
we are the parasites of the world
our job is to keep in step with the world.
The work of man is only just beginning
It remains for him to conquer
at the four corners of his fervour
every rigid prohibition.
No race holds a monopoly of beauty, intelligence and strength
there is room for all at the meeting-place of conquest
we know now
that the sun revolves round our earth illuminating the plot
which we alone have selected
that every star falls at our command from the sky to the earth
without limit or cease.

Aimé Césaire

UNE SAISON AU CONGO (fragment)

Lumumba Moi, sire, je pense aux oubliés. Nous sommes ceux
que l'on déposséda, que l'on frappa, que l'on mutila; ceux
que l'on tutoyait, ceux à qui l'on crachait au visage. Boys-
cuisine, boys-chambres, boys comme vous dites, lavadères,
nous fûmes un peuple de boys, un peuple de oui-bwana
et, qui doutait que l'homme pût ne pas être l'homme,
n'avait qu'à nous regarder.
   Sire, toute souffrance qui se pouvait souffrir, nous
l'avons soufferte. Toute humiliation qui se pouvait boire,
nous l'avons bue!
Mais, camarades, le goût de vivre, ils n'ont pu nous l'affadir dans
la bouche, et nous avons lutté, avec nos pauvres moyens
lutté pendant cinquante ans
et voici: nous avons vaincu.
Notre pays est désormais entre les mains de ses enfants.
Nôtre, ce ciel, ce fleuve, ces terres.
nôtre, le lac et la forêt.
nôtre, Karissimbi, Nyiragongo, Niamuragira, Mikéno,
Ehu, montagnes montées de la parole même du feu.
Congolais, aujourd'hui est un jour, grand.
C'est le jour où le monde accueille parmi les nations
Congo, notre mère
et surtout Congo, notre enfant,
l'enfant de nos veilles, de nos souffrances, de nos combats.
Camarades et frères de combat, que chacune de nos blessures
se transforme en mamelle!
Que chacune de nos pensées, chacune de nos espérances soit
rameau à brasser à neuf, l'air!
Pour Kongo! Tenez. Je l'élève au-dessus de ma tête;

Aimé Césaire

A SEASON IN THE CONGO (excerpt[1])

Lumumba As for me, Sire, my thoughts are for those who have been forgotten. We are the people who have been dispossessed, beaten, mutilated; the people whom the conquerors treated as inferiors, in whose faces they spat. A people of kitchen boys, house boys, laundry boys, in short, a people of boys, of yes-bwanas, and anyone who wanted to prove that a man is not necessarily a man could take us as an example.

Sire, whatever suffering, whatever humiliation could be known, we have known it.

But comrades, they were not able to dull our taste for life, and we resisted.

We didn't have much to fight with, but we fought, we fought for fifty years.

And today we have won.

Today our country is in the hands of its children.

This sky, this river, these lands are ours.

Ours the lake and the forest,

Ours Karissimbi, Nyiragongo, Niamuragira, Mikeno, Ehu, mountains sprung from the word of fire.

People of the Congo, this is a great day.

It is the day when the nations of the world welcome Congo our mother,

and still more Congo our child,

child of our sleepless nights, of our sufferings, of our struggles.

Comrades and brothers in combat, it is up to us to transform each of our wounds into a nurturing breast,

each of our thoughts, our hopes, into a fountain of change.

Kongo! Watch me. I raise him above my head;

---

[1]In Césaire's play, Lumumba, leader of the Congolese independence movement and now Prime Minister of the new state, makes this speech when his nation receives its independence from Belgium.

Je le ramène sur mon épaule
trois fois je lui crachote au visage
je le dépose par terre et vous demande à vous; en vérité,
connaissez-vous cet enfant? et vous répondez tous: c'est
Kongo, notre roi!
Je voudrais être toucan, le bel oiseau, pour être à travers le ciel,
annonceur, à races et langues que Kongo nous est né, notre
roi! Kongo, qu'il vive!
Kongo, tard né, qu'il suive l'épervier!
Kongo, tard né, qu'il clôture la palabre!
Camarades, tout est à faire, ou tout est à refaire, mais nous le
ferons, nous le referons. Pour Kongo!
Nous reprendrons les unes après les autres, toutes les lois, pour
Kongo!
Nous réviserons, les unes après les autres, toutes les coutumes,
pour Kongo!
Traquant l'injustice, nous reprendrons, l'une après l'autre toutes
les parties du vieil édifice, et du pied à la tête, pour Kongo!
Tout ce qui est courbé sera redressé, tout ce qui est dressé sera
rehaussé
pour Kongo!
Je demande l'union de tous!
Je demande le dévouement de tous! Pour Kongo! Uhuru!

Moment d'extase.

Congo! Grand Temps!
et nous, ayant brûlé de l'année oripeaux et défroques.
procédons de mon unanime pas jubilant
dans le temps neuf! Dans le solstice!

I put him back on my shoulder;

Three times I spit in his face;

I set him down on the ground, and I ask you; tell me the truth, do you know this child? And you all answer: it's Kongo, our king.

I wish I were a toucan, that wonderful bird, to cross the skies announcing to races and tongues that Kongo has been born to us, our king. Long live Kongo!

Kongo, late born, may he follow the sparrow hawk!

Kongo, late born, let him have the last word!

Comrades, everything remains to be done, or done over, but we will do it, we will do it over. For Kongo.

We will remake all the laws, one by one, for Kongo.

We will revise all the customs, one by one, for Kongo.

Uprooting injustice, we will rebuild the old edifice piece by piece, from cellar to attic, for Kongo.

That which is bowed shall be raised, and that which is raised shall be raised higher – for Kongo!

I demand the union of all.

I demand the devotion of every man. For Kongo!

Uhuru! Freedom!

A moment of ecstasy.

Congo! These are great days!

When this day's rags and this day's tinsel have been burned,

Let us advance rejoicing to my unanimous step

Into the new day! Into the solstice!

Aimé Césaire

HORS DES JOURS ÉTRANGERS

mon peuple

quand
hors des jours étrangers
germeras-tu une tête bien tienne sur tes épaules renouées
et ta parole

le congé dépêché aux traîtres
aux maîtres
le pain restitué la terre lavée
la terre donnée

quand
quand donc cesseras-tu d'être le jouet sombre
au carnaval des autres
ou dans les champs d'autrui
l'épouvantail désuet

demain
à quand demain mon peuple
la déroute mercenaire
finie la fête

mais la rougeur de l'est au coeur de balisier

peuple de mauvais sommeil rompu
peuple d'abîmes remontés
peuple de cauchemars domptés
peuple nocturne amant des fureurs du tonnerre

BEYOND FOREIGN DAYS

my people

when
beyond foreign days
will you sprout your very own head on your renewed shoulders
and your word

leave dispatched to traitors
to masters
bread restored the land washed
the land given

when
when will you finally cease being the somber plaything
at the carnival of others
or in the fields of another
the obsolete scarecrow

tomorrow
when is tomorrow my people
mercenaries put to flight
the party over

but the redness of the east in the heart of the balisier[1]

people trained to broken sleep
people of reconquered abysses
people of tamed nightmares
nocturnal people lovers of the thunder's fury

[1]Wild plantain tree.

demain plus haut plus doux plus large

et la houle torrentielle des terres
à la charrue salubre de l'orage

BARBARE

C'est le mot qui me soutient
et frappe sur ma carcasse de cuivre jaune
où la lune dévore dans la soupente de la rouille
les os barbares
des lâches bêtes rôdeuses du mensonge

Barbare
du langage sommaire
et nos faces belles comme le vrai pouvoir opératoire
de la négation

Barbare
des morts qui circulent dans les veines de la terre
et viennent se briser parfois la tête contre les murs de nos
oreilles
et les cris de révolte jamais entendus
qui tournent à mesure et à timbres de musique

Barbare
l'article unique

tomorrow higher softer wider

and the torrential surf of lands
plowed by the salubrious storm

BARBARIC

This is the word that sustains me
and strikes my brass carcass
where the moon devours in rusty garrets
the barbaric bones
of cowardly prowling lying beasts

Barbaric
of scant language
and our faces beautiful as the true operative power
of negation

Barbaric
the dead roaming in the veins of the earth
who sometimes come to smash their heads against the walls
      of our
ears
and the cries of revolt never heard
that turn to the measure and tone of the music

Barbaric
the single article

barbare le tapaya
barbare l'amphisbène blanche
barbare moi le serpent cracheur
qui de mes putréfiantes chairs me réveille
soudain gekko volant
soudain gekko frangé
et me colle si bien aux lieux mêmes de la force
qu'il vous faudra pour m'oublier
jeter aux chiens la chair velue de vos poitrines

MOT

Parmi moi
de moi-même
à moi-même
hors toute constellation
en mes mains serré seulement
le rare hoquet d'un ultime spasme délirant
vibre mot
j'aurai chance hors du labyrinthe
plus long plus large vibre
en ondes de plus en plus serrées
en lasso où me prendre
en corde où me pendre
et que me clouent toutes les flèches
et leur curare le plus amer
au beau poteau-mitan des très fraîches étoiles

barbaric the tapaya[1]
barbaric the white amphisbena[1]
barbaric me the spitting snake
waking from my putrefying flesh
suddenly a flying gecko[1]
suddenly a fringed gecko
and I cling so hard to the very places of strength
that to forget me you will have
to throw to the dogs the hairy flesh of your chests

WORD

Within me
of myself
to myself
beyond any constellation
in my hands clasped only
the rare hiccup of an ultimate delirious spasm
vibrates word
I'll have luck outside the labyrinth
longer wider vibrates
in tighter and tighter waves
in a lasso to seize me
in a rope to hang me
and nailed by all the arrows
and their most bitter curare[2]
to the dead-center pole of very cool stars

[1]All rare types of lizards.
[2]Poison for arrow tips.

vibre
vibre essence même de l'ombre
en aile en gosier c'est à force de périr
le mot nègre
sorti tout armé du hurlement
d'une fleur vénéneuse
le mot nègre
tout pouacre de parasites
le mot nègre
tout plein de brigands qui rôdent
des mères qui crient
d'enfants qui pleurent
le mot nègre
un grésillement de chairs qui brûlent
acre et de corne
le mot nègre
comme le soleil qui saigne de la griffe
sur le trottoir des nuages
le mot nègre
comme le dernier rire vêlé de l'innocence
entre les crocs du tigre
et comme le mot soleil est un claquement de balles
et comme le mot nuit un taffetas qu'on déchire
le mot nègre
        dru savez-vous
du tonnerre d'un été
      que s'arrogent
          des libertés incrédules

vibrates
vibrates the very essence of shadow
as a wing as a gullet enough to perish
the word Negro
extracted armed with a howl
from a venomous flower
the word Negro
lousy with parasites
the word Negro
full of brigands roaming
mothers screaming
children crying
the word Negro
a sizzling of flesh burning
with the acrid smell of horn
the word Negro
like the sun bleeding from the claw
on the sidewalk of the clouds
the word Negro
like the last calved laughter of innocence
between the tiger's fangs
and as the word sun is a snap of bullets
and the word night a tearing of taffeta
the word Negro
        tough you know
from the thunder of a summer
     claimed
           by incredulous liberties

Aimé Césaire

POUR SALUER LE TIERS MONDE

à Léopold Sédar Senghor

Ah!
mon demi-sommeil d'île si trouble
sur la mer!

Et voici de tous les points du péril
l'histoire qui me fait le signe que j'attendais,
Je vois pousser des nations.
Vertes et rouges, je vous salue,
bannières, gorges du vent ancien,
Mali, Guinée, Ghana

et je vous vois, hommes,
point maladroits sous ce soleil nouveau!

Écoutez:
de mon île lointaine
de mon île veilleuse
je vous dis Hoo!
Et vos voix me répondent
et ce qu'elles disent signifie:
«Il y fait clair». Et c'est vrai:
même à travers orage et nuit
pour nous il y fait clair.
D'ici je vois Kiwu vers Tanganika descendre
par l'escalier d'argent de la Ruzizi
(c'est la grande fille à chaque pas
baignant la nuit d'un frisson de cheveux)

Aimé Césaire

GREETINGS TO THE THIRD WORLD

à Léopold Sédar Senghor

Ah!
my half-sleep of a troubled island
on the sea!

And here from all the perilous points
history gives me the signal I was waiting for,
I see nations spring up.
Green and red, I salute you,
banners, gorges of the ancient wind,
Mali, Guinea, Ghana

and I see you, men,
not at all clumsy in this new sun!

Listen:
    from my remote island
    from my sleepy island
I say to you Hail!
    and your voices answer me
    and what they say means:
"Clear weather here." And it's true:
even through storm and night
for us it's clear weather there.
From here I see Kivu go to Tanganyika
down the silver staircase of the Ruzizi[1]
(she's the tall girl whose every step
bathes the night with a shudder of her hair)

[1]The Ruzizi River connects Lake Tanganyika to Lake Kivu.

d'ici, je vois noués
Bénoué, Logone et Tchad;
liés, Sénégal et Niger.
Rugir, silence et nuit rugir, d'ici j'entends
rugir le Nyaragongo.

De la haine, oui, ou le ban ou la barre
et l'arroi qui grunnit, mais
d'un roide vent, nous contus, j'ai vu
décroître la gueule négrière!

Je vois l'Afrique multiple et une
verticale dans la tumultueuse péripétie
avec ses bourrelets, ses nodules,
un peu à part, mais à portée
du siècle, comme un coeur de réserve.

Et je redis: Hoo mère!
      et je lève ma force
      inclinant ma face.
        Oh ma terre!
que je me l'émiette doucement entre pouce et index
que je m'en frotte la poitrine, le bras,
le bras gauche,
que je m'en caresse le bras droit.

Hoo ma terre est bonne,
     ta voix aussi est bonne
      avec cet apaisement que donne
       un lever de soleil!

Aimé Césaire

from here I see knotted
the Benue, the Logone and Chad
bound, the Senegal and the Niger[1]
Roar, silence and night roar, from here I hear
the Nyiragongo[2] roar.

Hatred, yes, or the ban or the bar
and the moaning plight, but
from the stiff wind that bruised us, I have seen
the face of slavery diminish!

I see Africa many and one
vertical in the tumultuous happenings
with her swellings, her bulges
somewhat apart, but within reach
of the century, like a heart in reserve.

And I repeat: Hail mother!
            and I lift my force
            bending my face.
                Oh my land!
let me crumble it gently between my thumb and index finger
let me rub it on my breast, my arm,
my left arm,
let me caress my right arm with it.

Hail my land is good,
        your voice too is good
        with that peacefulness given by
        a sunrise!

[1]Chad is a lake, the others are rivers.
[2]Volcano north of Lake Kivu.

Terre, forge et silo. Terre enseignant nos routes,
c'est ici, qu'une vérité s'avise,
taisant l'oripeau du vieil éclat cruel.

Vois:
    l'Afrique n'est plus
    au diamant du malheur
            un noir coeur qui se strie;

notre Afrique est une main hors du ceste,
c'est une main droite, la paume devant
et les doigts bien serrés;

c'est une main tuméfiée,
une-blessée-main-ouverte,
tendue,
        brunes, jaunes, blanches,
à toutes mains, à toutes les mains blessées
du monde.

Land, forge and silo. Land teaching us the way
it's here that a truth is asserted
dimming the ragged flag of the old cruel brilliance.

Look:
    Africa is no longer
    a black heart striped
        by the diamond of misfortune;

our Africa is a hand free of shackles
it's a right hand, palm outstretched
fingers close together;

it's a swollen hand
a-wounded-hand-open,
extended
    brown, yellow, white
to every hand, to every wounded hand
in the world.

Jacques Roumain

HAITI AND ITS POETS

Haiti, which shares the beautiful island of Hispaniola with the Dominican Republic, has had an especially bloody and violent history. Black slaves were imported to replace the million peaceful Arawak Indians who had died out by 1514 under the harsh treatment of the Spanish conquerors. In the seventeenth century, French buccaneers drove the Spaniards from the western part of the island, and the colony of Saint Domingue eventually became France's richest possession. A slave revolt, led by Toussaint Louverture, resulted in the country's independence in 1804 and the foundation of the only Black republic in the New World — now called Haiti, the original Arawak name of the island. A tumultuous succession of presidents and insurrections in the nineteenth century further depleted the ravaged land. Despite this turmoil, poetry flourished, influenced by the Romantic, Parnassian, and Symbolist schools of France. In 1915, the U.S. Marines occupied the country, adding to the indignation of the younger poets, who, inspired by the ethnological studies of Jean Price-Mars, diplomat and doctor, had begun to look into their African patrimony. Indigenous songs, legends, proverbs, and beliefs such as voodoo, a syncretic religion of African and Christian liturgy, inspired their material rather than the works of French writers. And so after 1920 Haitian poetry became Black. By 1958 the repressive Duvalier regime had driven most of Haiti's poets into exile.

Jacques Roumain

BOIS-D'ÉBÈNE (fragments)

Voici pour ta voix un écho de chair et de sang
noir messager d'espoir
car tu connais tous les chants du monde
depuis ceux des chantiers immémoriaux du Nil

Tu te souviens de chaque mot le poids des pierres d'Égypte
et l'élan de ta misère a dressé les colonnes des temples
comme un sanglot de sève la tige des roseaux

Cortège titubant ivre de mirages
sur la piste des caravanes d'esclaves
élèvent
maigres branchages d'ombres enchaînés de soleil
des bras implorants vers nos dieux

Mandingue Arada Bambara Ibo
gémissant un chant qu'étranglaient les carcans
(et quand nous arrivâmes à la côte
Mandingue Bambara Ibo
quand nous arrivâmes à la côte

Jacques Roumain (1907-1944), the aristocratic novelist, journalist, anthropologist, and poet, was educated in Europe but at 20 returned to Haiti where he became a leader of the Indigenist movement. His poetic peasant novel *Governors of the Dew* expresses his Marxist vision. The following excerpt is from the long poem "Ebony Wood."

EBONY WOOD[1] (excerpts)

Here for your voice is an echo of flesh and blood
black messenger of hope
for you have known all the songs in the world
since those of the Nile's immemorial building sites

You remember with every word the weight of the
    Egyptian stones
and the thrust of your misery raised columns of temples
like a sigh of sap the stem of reeds

Staggering cortege drunk with mirages
on the trail of the slave caravans
raising
thin branches of shadows linked by the sun
of arms imploring our gods

Mandingo Arada Bambara Ibo[2]
groaning a chant strangled by iron collars
(and when we arrived at the coast
Mandingo Bambara Ibo
when we arrived at the coast

[1]In colloquial French, *bois d'ébène* may mean "black ivory," i.e., the Negro slave trade.
[2]West African tribes sold into slavery.

Jacques Roumain

Bambara Ibo
il ne restait de nous
Bambara Ibo
qu'une poignée de grains épars
dans la main du semeur de mort)

Ce même chant repris aujourd'hui au Congo
Mais quand donc ô mon peuple
les hivers en flamme dispersant un orage
d'oiseaux de cendre
reconnaîtrai-je la révolte de tes mains?

Et que j'écoutai aux Antilles
car ce chant négresse
qui t'enseigna négresse ce chant d'immense
peine
négresse des Iles négresse des plantations
cette plainte désolée

Comme dans la conque le souffle oppressé des mers

Mais je sais aussi un silence
un silence de vingt-cinq mille cadavres nègres
de vingt-cinq mille traverses de Bois-d'Ébène

Sur les rails du Congo-Océan
mais je sais
des suaires de silence aux branches des cyprès
des pétales de noirs caillots aux ronces
de ce bois où fut lynché mon frère de Géorgie

. . . . .

Bambara Ibo
there was left of us
Bambara Ibo
only a handful of scattered seeds
in the hand of the sower of death)

This same chant taken up again today in the Congo
But when oh my people
winters in flames scattering a storm
of birds of ashes
shall I recognize the revolt of your hands?

And I heard it in the Antilles
this negress chant
who taught you Negress this chant of immense
pain
Negress of the islands Negress of the plantations
this desolate plea

As in the seashell the oppressed breathing of the seas

But I know too a silence
a silence of twenty-five thousand Negro corpses
of twenty-five thousand ties of Ebony Wood

On the tracks of the Congo-Ocean railroad
but I know
shrouds of silence on the cypress branches
petals of black clots in the brambles
in the woods of Georgia where my brother was lynched

. . . . .

Jacques Roumain

le silence

plus déchirant qu'un simoun de sagaies
plus rugissant qu'un cyclone de fauves
et qui hurle
s'élève
appelle
vengeance et châtiment
un raz de marée de pus et de lave
sur la félonie du monde
et le tympan du ciel crevé sous le poing
de la justice

Afrique j'ai gardé ta mémoire Afrique
tu es en moi

Comme l'écharde dans la blessure
comme un fétiche tutélaire au centre du village
fais de moi la pierre de ta fronde
de ma bouche les lèvres de ta plaie
de mes genoux les colonnes brisées de ton abaissement . . .

　　POURTANT
je ne veux être que de votre race
ouvriers paysans de tous les pays
ce qui nous sépare
les climats l'étendue l'espace
les mers
un peu de mousse de voiliers dans un baquet d'indigo
une lessive de nuages séchant sur l'horizon
ici des chaumes un impur marigot
là des steppes tondues aux ciseaux du gel

the silence

more lacerating than a simoon[1] of spears
more roaring than a cyclone of wild beasts
and that bellows
rises up
calls for
vengeance and punishment
a tidal wave of pus and lava
over the felony of the world
and the sky's ear-drum punctured under the fist
of justice

Africa I have kept your memory
you are in me

Like the splinter in the wound
like a guardian fetish in the center of the village
make of me the stone of your slingshot
of my mouth the lips of your wound
of my knees the broken columns of your abasement . . .

    YET
I want to be only of your race
workers peasants of all countries
what separates us
climates expanse space
seas
a little sailboat spray in a bucket of indigo
a wash of clouds drying on the horizon
here thatched roofs an impure swamp
there steppes tonsured by scissors of frost

[1]A hot dry violent wind laden with dust from the African desert.

des alpages
la rêverie d'une prairie bercée de peupliers
le collier d'une rivière à la gorge d'une colline
le pouls des fabriques martelant la fièvre des étés
d'autres plages d'autres jungles
l'assemblée des montagnes
habitée de la haute pensée des éperviers
d'autres villages

Est-ce tout cela climat étendue espace
qui crée le clan la tribu la nation
la peau la race et les dieux
notre dissemblance inexorable?

Jean-F. Brièrre

ME REVOICI, HARLEM

Au souvenir des lynchés de Géorgie
victimes du fascisme blanc.

Frère Noir, me voici ni moins pauvre que toi,
Ni moins triste ou plus grand. Je suis parmi la foule
L'anonyme passant qui grossit le convoi,
La goutte noire solidaire de tes houles.

mountain pastures
the dreaminess of a prairie cradled by poplars
the necklace of a river at the throat of a hill
the pulse of factories hammering the fever of summers
other beaches other jungles
the assembly of mountains
inhabited by the lofty thought of sparrow-hawks
other villages

Is that all climate expanse space
which creates the clan the tribe the nation
the skin the race the gods
our inexorable dissimilarity?

Jean-F. Brièrre (born 1909) was imprisoned and exiled by the Duvalier regime after a distinguished career in government and literature. He lived in Jamaica and then in Dakar, where he worked in the Senegalese Ministry of Cultural Affairs. "Harlem," written in 1944, reflects the growing solidarity with American Blacks felt by the poets of Negritude.

HERE I AM, HARLEM

In memory of the lynched in Georgia
victims of white fascism.

Black Brother, here I am no less poor than you,
No less sad or more great, I am part of the crowd
The anonymous passer-by who fattens the convoy,
The fraternal black drop within your sea swell.

Jean-F. Brièrre

Vois, tes mains ne sont pas moins noires que nos mains,
Et nos pas à travers des siècles de misère
Marquent le même glas sur le même chemin:
Nos ombres s'enlaçaient aux marches des calvaires.

Car nous avons déjà côte à côte lutté.
Lorsque je trébuchais, tu ramassais mes armes,
Et de tout ton grand corps par le labeur sculpté,
Tu protégeais ma chute et souriais en larmes.

De la jungle montait un silence profond
Que brisaient par moments d'indicibles souffrances.
Dans l'âcre odeur du sang je relevais le front
Et te voyais dressé sur l'horizon, immense.

Nous connûmes tous deux l'horreur des négriers . . .
Et souvent comme moi tu sens des courbatures
Se réveiller après les siècles meurtriers,
Et saigner dans ta chair les anciennes blessures.

Mais il fallut nous dire adieu vers seize cent.
Nous eûmes un regard où dansaient des mirages,
D'épiques visions de bataille et de sang:
Je revois ta silhouette aux ténèbres des âges.

Ta trace se perdit aux rives de l'Hudson.
L'été à Saint-Domingue accueillit mon angoisse,
Et l'écho me conta dans d'étranges chansons
Les Peaux-Rouges pensifs dont on défit la race.

Jean-F. Brièrre

See, your hands are no less black than our hands,
And our footsteps across centuries of misery
Strike the same death knell on the same path:
Our shadows are entwined on calvaries' steps.

For we have already fought side by side.
When I stumbled, you took up my arms,
And with your whole great body by labor sculpted,
You blocked my fall and smiled through tears.

From the jungle arose a profound silence
Broken occasionally by unutterable suffering.
In the bitter odor of blood I lifted my head
and saw you pitched against the horizon, immense.

We both knew the horror of slavers . . .
And often like me you feel stiffness
Awaken after murderous centuries
And ancient wounds bleeding in your flesh.

But we had to say good-bye around sixteen hundred.
We exchanged a glance in which mirages danced,
Of epic visions of battle and blood:
I see your silhouette again in the darkness of the ages.

Your trace was lost on the banks of the Hudson.
Summer in Saint Domingue[1] greeted my anguish,
And echoes told the tale in strange songs
Of pensive Redskins whose race was defied.

[1] The French name for the colony that is now Haiti.

Jean-F. Brièrre

Les siècles ont changé de chiffres dans le temps.
Saint-Domingue, brisant les chaînes, les lanières,
— L'incendie étalant sa toile de titan —
Arbora son drapeau sanglant dans la lumière.

Me revoici, Harlem. Ce Drapeau, c'est le tien,
Car le pacte d'orgueil, de gloire et de souffrance,
Nous l'avons contracté pour hier et demain:
Je déchire aujourd'hui les suaires du silence.

Ton carcan blesse encor mon cri le plus fécond.
Comme hier dans la cale aux sombres agonies,
Ton appel se déchire aux barreaux des prisons,
Et je respire mal lorsque tu t'asphyxies.

Nous avons désappris le dialecte africain,
Tu chantes en anglais mon rêve et ma souffrance,
Au rythme de tes blues dansent mes vieux chagrins,
Et je dis ton angoisse en la langue de France.

Le mépris qu'on te jette est sur ma joue à moi.
Le Lynché de Floride a son ombre en mon âme,
Et du bûcher sanglant que protège la loi,
Vers ton coeur, vers mon coeur monte la même flamme.

Quand tu saignes, Harlem, s'empourpre mon mouchoir.
Quand tu souffres, ta plante en mon chant se prolonge.
De la même ferveur et dans le même soir,
Frère Noir, nous faisons tous deux le même songe.

Jean-F. Brièrre

The centuries have changed statistics in time.
Saint Domingue, breaking the chains, the lashes,
— Fire stretching its titan's canvas —
Hoisted its bloody flag in the light.

Here I am, Harlem. That Flag is yours,
For the pact of pride, of glory, and of suffering,
We made it for yesterday and tomorrow:
Today I rip apart the shrouds of silence.

Your iron collar still cuts into my most fertile scream.
As it did yesterday in the ship's hold of somber agonies,
Your cry is shredded by prison bars,
And I have trouble breathing while you smother.

We have unlearned African dialect,
You sing my dream and my suffering in English,
My old worries dance to the rhythm of your blues,
And I speak your anguish in the language of France.

The contempt they hurl at you hits my cheeks too.
The man lynched in Florida has his shadow in my soul,
And from the bloody pyre protected by the law,
The same flame leaps toward your heart, toward my heart.

When you bleed, Harlem, my handkerchief turns crimson.
When you suffer, your groan is prolonged in my song.
With the same fervor and in the same night,
Black Brother, we both have the same dream.

René Depestre

ON LES RECONNAÎT

Dans tous les lieux du monde
on les reconnaît
au lait qui coule de leurs rires.

On les reconnaît
à leur coeur rompu
à leurs muscles sans repos.

On les reconnaît
à leurs jambes déliées
à leurs poings de dur métal
aux rossignols qui nichent dans leur gosier

Dans tous les lieux du monde
Nègres de triste saison.

ALABAMA

Si j'ai une fille je ne l'appellerai pas Alabama,
Je ne donnerai pas ce nom au cerisier qui vient de naître
près de ma maison,

René Depestre (born 1926) is perhaps the most renowned and
prolific of contemporary Haitian poets. A communist and,
like many others, an exile, he has most recently lived in
Cuba. His odes to Lumumba and Malcolm X are from *A
Rainbow for the Christian West,* a collection whose
structure is based on voodoo liturgy.

YOU RECOGNIZE THEM

In all the places of the world
you recognize them
by the milk that flows from their laughter.

You recognize them
by their broken heart
by their unrested muscles.

You recognize them
by their loose limbs
by their hard metallic fists
by the nightingales nesting in their throats.

In all the places of the world
Negroes of sad season.

ALABAMA

If I have a daughter I won't call her Alabama,
I won't give that name to the new-born cherry tree
near my house,

Ni au grand bateau que je lance parfois sur les eaux
      intérieures de ma tendresse.
Alabama, je ne nommerai pas ainsi la joie qui dans les
       yeux parisiens de Suzanne cherchait toujours à
      mordre ma joie.
Alabama, je n'écrirai pas ce mot sur l'oreiller d'un
      enfant malade,
Ni sur l'horizon d'un prisonnier innocent,
Ni sur les hauts murs de ma tristesse.
Alabama, ce n'est pas un nom pour la première école
      de ton village natal,
Ce n'est pas un nom pour un pont, un train, une
      boulangerie.

Jadis je pouvais imaginer le mot Alabama
Ecrit sur le front d'une grande danseuse
Ou sur la porte d'un fabricant de poupées.
Maintenant nul au monde ne peut l'écrire
Sur les vitres de la santé ou de l'espoir.
Alabama, c'est le nom que je lis sur les chaînes de
      mes frères noirs,
C'est le nom que je lis sur leurs lampes brisées.
Et si ma main droite s'appelait aussi Alabama
Je devrais cette nuit même la couper
Pour pouvoir écrire encore des poèmes à la gloire
      des hommes.

                              Mai 1963

Nor to the great boat that I sometimes launch on the
      private waters of my tenderness.
Alabama, I won't so name the joy in Suzanne's Parisian
      eyes that always sought to bite my joy.
Alabama, I won't write that word on a sick child's pillow,
Nor on an innocent prisoner's horizon,
Nor on the high walls of my sadness,
Alabama is no name for the first school in your
      native village,
It's no name for a bridge, a train, a bakery.

Once upon a time I could imagine the word Alabama
Written on the forehead of a great dancer
Or on the door of a doll manufacturer.
Now no one in the world can write it
On the windowpanes of health or hope.
Alabama, it's the name I read on the chains of my
      black brothers,
It's the name I read on their broken lamps.
And if my right hand was also called Alabama
I would have to cut it off this very night
So I could still write poems to the glory of men.

May 1963

ODE À PATRICE LUMUMBA

Simbi

Moi la tête toujours jeune de l'eau
Moi le ventre ébloui de l'eau
Qui vient rafraîchir son visage à même la source de
      mes mains?
Quel autre palmier royal de notre race va poser sa soif
      d'Afrique sur mes genoux?
O Afrique patiente et bonne sous ma rosée
Afrique combattante d'Alger jusqu'au Cap
En ce temps de mes noces avec ta révolte
En ce temps du vivre les armes à la main
C'est Patrice Lumumba que je plonge dans la fraîcheur
      de nos îles vertes!

Regardez-le ce coq-tempête du Congo
Tous les malheurs de l'Afrique sont peints sur les murs
      de son âme: un tatouage fantastique de mensonges
      et d'atrocités
Patrice cherchait la beauté pour les jours et les nuits
      du Congo
Il trouva toutes sortes de rois étrangers
Qui font couler devant leurs portes
Des congos de diamant et de cuivre
Des congos de bauxite et d'uranium
Il trouva des chiffres menaçants
Des chiffres-tigres des Bourses-panthères
Des titres en baisse ou en hausse selon que la joie monte
      ou descend au coeur du Congo
Il trouva l'UNION-MINIERE-DU-HAUT-KATANGA
Le plus féroce serpent d'Afrique!

René Depestre

ODE TO PATRICE LUMUMBA

Simbi[1]

I the ever young head of the water
I the dazzled belly of the water
Who comes to cool his face at the very spring of
      my hands?
What other royal palm tree of our race is going to put his
      African thirst in my lap?
O Africa patient and good under my dew
Africa embattled from Algiers to the Cape
In this time of my wedding with your revolt
In this time of armed living
It's Patrice Lumumba whom I plunge into the coolness
      of our green islands!

Look at him this hurricane-cock from the Congo
All of Africa's misfortunes are painted on the walls of his
      soul: a fantastic tattoo of lies and atrocities
Patrice sought beauty for the days and the nights of
      the Congo
He found all sorts of foreign kings
Who had flowing before their doors
congos of diamond and copper
congos of bauxite and uranium
He found threatening figures
Tiger-figures of panther-stock markets
Stocks going up or down depending on whether joy is
      high or low in the heart of the Congo
He found THE MINING UNION OF UPPER KATANGA
The most ferocious snake in Africa!

[1]Female guardian of the waters in Haitian peasant mythology.

73

Le voici avec sa gueule qui s'ouvre comme un abîme avec
     ses eaux déchaînées avec ses écumes verdâtres
Il annonce la mort violente
C'est un dieu sauvage, cruel, obscène qui signe ses
     crimes U.M.H.K.
C'est un loa milliardaire que se nourrit seulement de
     métal arrosé de sang d'homme noir
Tout ce qui coupe tout ce qui empoisonne
Tout ce qui dessèche et tue le doux chant de l'homme
Est du ressort de ce grand sorcier d'Occident!

Patrice avance vers sa lave géante
Toute la force du Congo est dans ses yeux
Il avance les mains nues, le coeur pur
Son enfance brille encor dans ses mots
Mais soudain son innocence découvre
Le-nègre-écorcheur-et-vendeur-de-nègres
Le-nègre-tonton-macoute-le-nègre-attaché-au-nombril-
     impur-de-l'Occident
Le-nègre-petit-chien-hystérique-des-salons-d'Europe-
     et-d'Amérique
Le-nègre-colporteur-de-lâchetés
Le-nègre-atteint-de-la-mauvaise-fièvre-Tschombé!

Il est déjà trop tard. Déjà la négraille d'espèce rampante
Vend avec ardeur des actions sur chaque goutte de
     sang lumumbien

There it is with its mouth opening like an abyss with
    its juices unleashed with its greenish foam
It announces violent death
It's a savage, cruel, obscene god who signs his
    crimes M.U.U.K.
It's a billionaire loa[1] who feeds only on metal sprayed
    with the black man's blood
Everything that cuts everything that poisons
Everything that dries up and kills the sweet song of man
Springs from this great witch-doctor of the West!

Patrice goes to meet its giant lava
All the Congo's strength is in his eyes
He advances bare-handed pure-hearted
His childhood still shines in his words
But suddenly his innocence discovers
The-Negro-flayer-and-seller-of-Negroes
The-Negro-tonton-macoute[2]-the-Negro-tied-to-the
    impure-navel-of-the-West
The-hysterical-toy-poodle-Negro-of-the-drawing-rooms-
    of-Europe-and-America
The-Negro-peddlar-of-cowardice
The-Negro-gripped-by-evil-fever-Tshombe[3]!

It's already too late. Already filthy niggers of the
    crawling kind
Are zestfully selling shares of each drop of Lumumbian
    blood

[1]A voodoo divinity — some are evil, some are good spirits.

[2]Haitian secret police of Duvalier.

[3]President of the secessionist state of Katanga, the mineral-rich province containing the bulk of the Congo's wealth. Its secession brought about civil war in the Congo (1960) right after independance from Belgium and toppled Lumumba, who was eventually assassinated. It is generally agreed that Tshombe was the tool of European financial interests.

Des actions sur ses os, ses glandes, ses viscères
Des actions sur sa voix, ses regards tendres
Et des actions sur les anges végétaux
Qui parfois sanglotaient dans son âme !

Ainsi l'Afrique le vit passer
Dans la fumée de son combat
Un nègre-phare un nègre-étoile
Un nègre-arbre-fruitier
Qui dépassait d'un feuillage
Les plus hautes vagues de la mer
Et l'invincible tendresse des hommes !

ODE À MALCOLM X

Grande Brigitte

Il était une fois un nègre de Harlem
Il haïssait l'alcool et les cigarettes
Il haïssait le mensonge et le vol et les Blancs
Sa sagesse venait de la chaux vive
Sa vérité brillait comme un rasoir
Né pour la douceur et la bonté il
Préchait que l'enfer c'était l'homme blanc
Et un soir le voici tout seul avec sa haine
Avec ses prophéties et sa grande tristesse
Il pense que peut-être tous les Blancs
Ne sont pas des loups et des serpents
Et il pleure Malcolm X l'agneau de Harlem

Shares of his bones, his glands, his viscera
Shares of his voice, his tender looks
And shares of the vegetal angels
Who sometime sob in his soul!

So Africa saw him pass
In the smoke of her combat
A Negro-lighthouse a Negro-star
A Negro-fruit-tree
Who was taller by a leafy branch than
The highest waves of the sea
And the invincible tenderness of men!

ODE TO MALCOM X

Big Brigitte[1]

Once upon a time there was a Negro of Harlem
He hated alcohol and cigarettes
He hated lies and theft and Whites
His wisdom came from quicklime
His truth shone like a razor
Born for sweetness and kindness he
Preached that hell was the white man
And one evening there he is all alone with his hatred
With his prophecies and his great sadness
He thinks that maybe all Whites
Aren't wolves and snakes
And he weeps Malcolm X the lamb of Harlem

[1]Another participant in the voodoo ritual.

Il remonte en pleurant les rues de son enfance
Et il remonte encor plus loin dans le passé
Ses larmes traversent le temps et les pays
Elles coulent avec les fleuves les plus vieux
Elles coulent sur les murs de Jérusalem
Et se mêlent aux légendes les plus vieilles
Elles font le tour de la Bible et du Coran
Qui deviennent des îles au fond de sa douleur
Se lève le soleil sur Harlem et Malcolm
Suit encore l'aventure de ses larmes
Ensuite il s'habille, prend un verre de lait
Et sort dans la rue conter l'histoire du monde:
« J'accuse l'homme blanc d'être un semeur de haine! »
Et six balles aussitôt se jettent sur sa vie...
Il était Malcolm X un nègre-rayon qui
Haïssait les larmes les chaînes et la haine!

Anthony Phelps

MON PAYS QUE VOICI (fragments)

Car un matin ils sont venus
ces caraïbes d'une autre race
anthropophages
à leur façon

He walks weeping down the streets of Harlem
And he walks still further down the past
His tears cross over time and countries
They flow with the oldest rivers
They flow along the walls of Jerusalem
And mingle with the oldest legends
They tour through the Bible and the Koran
That become islands in the depths of his sorrow
Rises the sun on Harlem and Malcolm
Follows still the adventure of his tears
Then he dresses, has a glass of milk
And goes out in the street to tell the story of the world:
"I accuse the white man of sowing hatred!"
And six bullets are hurled at his life . . .
He was Malcolm X a Negro-ray-of-light who
Hated tears chains and hatred!

Anthony Phelps (born 1928) studied chemistry in the U.S. After being imprisoned by Duvalier, he went into exile in 1964, in Montreal, where he has resumed his theatrical and journalistic career. The following passages are excerpted from his long epic poem on Haiti's history, which Phelps has recorded on his own "Disques Coumbite" label.

THIS IS MY COUNTRY (excerpts)

For one morning they came
those Caribes[1] of another race
man-eating
in their fashion

[1]The warlike Indian tribe who inhabited the Caribbean before the arrival of the Europeans and who gave the region its name.

Car un matin ils sont venus
par la route salée et les chemins de sable
à la recherche de leur dieu
le pur métal aux reflets jaunes

Et ils sont morts ô mon Pays
tes premiers fils
au fond des mines
pour que les grands aient couche molle
et vaisseaux bien gréés
. . . . .

Je continue ma lente marche dans les ténèbres
car c'est le règne des vaisseaux de mort

Ils sont venus à fond de cale
tes nouveaux fils à la peau noire
pour la relève de l'indien au fond des mines
(Le dieu de l'Espagnol n'a point de préjugés
pourvu que ses grands lieux de pierres et de prières
soient rehaussés de sa présence aux reflets jaunes
peu lui importe la main qui le remonte
du ventre de la terre)
Et l'homme noir est arrivé
avec sa force et sa chanson
Il était prêt pour la relève
et prêt aussi pour le dépassement
Sa peau tannée défia la trique et le supplice
Son corps de bronze n'était pas fait pour l'esclavage
car s'il était couleur d'ébène
c'est qu'il avait connu la grande plaine
brûlée de Liberté
. . . . .

Or un matin
le dieu de l'Espagnol

For one morning they came
by the salty route and the sandy paths
looking for their god
the pure metal with yellow reflections

And they died oh my Country
your first sons
in the depths of the mines
so the grandees might have a soft bed
and well-rigged ships
          .   .   .   .   .

I continue my slow march in darkness
for it's the reign of the death ships

They came in the bottom of the hold
your new black-skinned sons
to replace the Indian in the depths of the mines
(The Spaniard's god has no prejudices
provided his great places of stones and prayers
gleam with his presence of yellow reflections
he's indifferent to the hand that brings it up
from the belly of the earth)
And the black man arrived
with his strength and his song
He was ready to replace
and ready too for overreaching
His tanned skin defied cudgel and torment
His bronze body wasn't made for slavery
he was color of ebony
because he had known the great burned
plain of Liberty
          .   .   .   .   .

Then one morning
the Spaniard's god

trouva d'autres adorateurs
et qui s'en vinrent
par la porte mouvante
avec en main le tissu étoilé
et dans la bouche une langue inconnue

. . . . .

En vain sur une porte
fut crucifié Charlemagne Péralte
Et les cinq mille cacos
en vain donnèrent leur sang
par toutes leurs blessures

Le dieu vert des yankees était plus fort que les loas

Et tout fut à recommencer
selon le rythme de leur vie
selon leurs lois leurs préjugés

Et tout fut à recommencer
car un matin ils sont venus
ces protecteurs vêtus de jaune
nous enseigner avec la honte
la délation et la servilité

Et la leçon fut profitable
car dans ma lente marche de Poète
j'ai vu ô mon Pays tes enfants sans mémoire
dans toutes les capitales de l'Amérique
le coui tendu et toute fierté bue
genoux ployés devant le dieu-papier
à l'effigie de Washington

found other worshipers
and they came by the moving gate
holding a starry cloth
and in their mouths an unknown tongue

· · · · ·

In vain on a door
was Charlemagne Péralte crucified
And the five thousand "cacos"[1]
in vain gave blood
through all their wounds

The yankees' green god was stronger than the loas[2]

And everything had to begin again
according to their rhythm of life
according to their laws their prejudices

And everything had to begin again
for one morning they came
these protectors dressed in yellow
to teach us along with shame
betrayal and servility

And the lesson was profitable
for in my slow Poet's march
I have seen oh my Country your children without memory
in all the capitals of America
panhandling all pride swallowed
knees bent before the paper god
in the effigy of Washington[3]

---

[1]Peasants who revolted under the American occupation. Péralte was one of
 their leaders.
[2]Voodoo divinities.
[3]The dollar bill.

Anthony Phelps

A quoi bon ce passé de douleurs et de gloire
et à quoi bon dix huit cent quatre

O mon Pays je t'aime comme un être de chair
et je sais ta souffrance et je vois ta misère
et me demande la rage au coeur
quelle main a tracé sur le registre des nations
une petite étoile à côté de ton nom

Yankee de mon coeur
qui bois mon café
et mon cacao
qui pompes la sève
de ma canne à sucre

Yankee de mon coeur
qui entres chez moi
en pays conquis
imprimes ma gourde
et bats ma monnaie

Yankee de mon coeur
qui viens dans ma caille
parler en anglais
Qui changes le nom
de mes vieilles rues

Yankee de mon coeur
j'attends dans ma nuit
que le vent change d'aire

· · · · ·

Anthony Phelps

What good is this past of sorrow and glory
and what good is eighteen hundred four[1]

Oh my Country I love you as if you were of flesh
and I know your suffering and I see your misery
and wonder, rage in my heart,
what hand on the register of nations drew
a small star beside your name

Yankee of my heart
who drinks my coffee
and my cocoa
who pumps the sap
of my sugar cane

Yankee of my heart
who enters my home
as a conquered country
prints my "gourde"[2]
and mints my coins

Yankee of my heart
who comes into my shack
to speak in English
who changes the name
of my old streets

Yankee of my heart
I wait in my night
for the wind to change direction

· · · · ·

[1]Date of Haitian independence from France.
[2]Haitian currency.

Louis "Satchmo" Armstrong

TWO POETS FROM GUADELOUPE

Guadeloupe is another overseas department of France and like Martinique, it is a poor, volcanic island. Paul Niger and Guy Tirolien were both born there in 1917; both were educated in Paris and associated with the magazine *Presence Africaine,* and both pursued literary and government careers in Black Africa.

Niger, a novelist and poet, was born Paul Béville, but he adopted the name of the African river. The following excerpt from his long poem "I don't like Africa" expresses the Black man's horror at the exploitative French neo-colonial policy, which he observed at close hand as an administrator for the French government in Dahomey. He died in 1962 in a plane crash returning from Guadeloupe, just as Black Africa was becoming independent.

Guy Tirolien was also an overseas administrator of the French government in Cameroon and the Sudan. Since African independence, he has worked for the government of Niger and as the U.N. representative to Mali. His earlier poems are marvelous reflections of his childhood in Guadeloupe. "Satchmo" was chosen for inclusion here for its celebration of an American Black hero.

Paul Niger

JE N'AIME PAS L'AFRIQUE (fragment)

J'aime ce pays, disait-il; on y trouve:
> «Nourriture, obéissance, poulets à quatre sous,
> femmes à cent,
> et «bien Missié» pour pas plus cher.

Le seul problème, ajoutait-il, ce sont les anciens tirailleurs
> et les métis et les lettrés qui discutent les ordres
> et veulent se faire élire chefs de village.»

Moi, je n'aime pas cette Afrique-là.

L'Afrique des «naya»
L'Afrique des «makou»
L'Afrique des «a bana»
L'Afrique des yesmen et des beni-oui-oui
L'Afrique des hommes couchés attendant comme une grâce
> le réveil de la botte
L'Afrique des boubous flottant comme des drapeaux de capitu-
> lation, de la dysenterie, de la peste, de la fièvre jaune et des
> chiques (pour ne pas dire de la chicote).

L'Afrique de «l'homme du Niger», l'Afrique des plaines désolées
Labourées d'un soleil homicide, l'Afrique des pagnes obscènes
> et des muscles noués par l'effort du travail forcé,

I DON'T LIKE AFRICA (excerpt)

I like this country, he said; you find here:
>"Food, obedience, chicken for a nickel, women for a dollar,
>and 'yassuh' for not much more.

The only problem, he added, are the veteran sharpshooters and
>the half-breeds and those who can read who dispute orders
>and want to be elected village chiefs."

Personally, I don't like that Africa.

The Africa of the "naya"[1]
The Africa of the "makou"[2]
The Africa of the "a bana"[3]
The Africa of the yesmen and the beni-oui-oui
The Africa of men lying down awaiting like a blessing
>the awakening of the boot
The Africa of boubous[4] floating like flags of capitulation,
>of dysentry, of plague, of yellow fever, of chiggers
>(not to mention the lash.)

The Africa of "The Man from Niger,"[5] the Africa of desolate
>plains
Ploughed by a homicidal sun, the Africa of obscene loin-cloths
>and muscles knotted by the effort of forced labor,

[1]Here.
[2]Silence.
[3]Finished.
[4]A tunic-like article of clothing.
[5]A French colonial film.

Paul Niger

L'Afrique des négresses servant l'alcool d'oubli sur le plateau
    de leurs lèvres,
L'Afrique des boys suceurs, des maîtresses de douze ans,
des seins au balancement rythmé de papayes trop mûres
et des ventres ronds comme une calebasse en saison sèche,

Je n'aime pas cette Afrique-là.

Dieu, un jour descendu sur la terre, fut désolé de l'attitude des
    créatures envers la création. Il ordonna le déluge, et, de la
    terre resurgie, une semence nouvelle germa.
L'arche peupla le monde et lentement
Lentement
L'humanité monta des âges sans lumière aux âges sans repos.

Il avait oublié l'Afrique.

Christ racheta l'homme mauvais et bâtit son Eglise à Rome.
Sa voix fut entendue dans le désert. L'Eglise sur la Société,
la Société sur l'Eglise, l'une portant l'autre,
Fondèrent la civilisation où les hommes, dociles à l'antique
    sagesse,
pour apaiser les anciens dieux, pas morts,
Immolèrent tous les dix ans quelques milliers de victimes

    Il avait oublié l'Afrique.

Mais quand on s'aperçut qu'une race (d'hommes?)
Devait encore à Dieu son tribut de sang noir on lui fit un rappel
Elle solda.
Et solde encore. Et lorsqu'elle demanda sa place au sein de
    l'oecumène on lui désigna quelques bancs. Elle s'assit. Et
    s'endormit.

The Africa of Negresses serving the alcohol of mindlessness on
    the tray of their lips.
The Africa of cocksucking "boys," of twelve-year-old mistresses,
breasts of overripe papayas swaying in rhythm
and bellies round as a calabash in the dry season.

I don't like that Africa.

God, one day descended to earth, was stricken by the attitude
    of creatures toward creation. He ordered the Flood, and
    from the reborn earth, a new seed sprouted.
The ark peopled the world and slowly
Slowly
Humanity climbed from the ages without light to the ages
    without rest.

He had forgotten Africa.

Christ redeemed wicked man and built his Church in Rome.
His voice was heard in the desert. The Church on Society,
Society on the Church, one carrying the other,
Founded civilization where men, docile to the ancient wisdom,
to appease the ancient gods, not dead,
Immolated several thousand victims every ten years

    He had forgotten Africa.

But when it was noticed that a race (of men?)
Still owed God a tribute of black blood, they were called to order
They paid off.
And are still paying off. And when they demand a place in the
    bosom of the ecumenical council they are shown to a few
    benches. They sit down. And fall asleep.

Paul Niger

Jésus étendit les mains sur ces têtes frisées et les nègres furent
    sauvés.

Pas ici-bas, bien sûr.

. . . . .

Guy Tirolien

SATCHMO

non
ne fermez pas l'oreille
aux hoquets aux sanglots
aux subtils glissandos
à la stridence à l'insistance
à la cadence
des blues
      — swingués oh!
          par la trompette de Satchmo

plainte étouffée dans le gosier
du noir lynché

glouglou du sang
glissant
sur les courants puissants
        du fleuve
          Mississippi

Jesus stretched his hands over these curly heads and the Negroes
    were saved.

Not here on earth, of course.

                    .   .   .   .   .

SATCHMO

No
don't shut your ears
to the hiccups to the sobs
to the subtle glissandos
to the stridence to the insistence
to the cadence
of the blues
        —swung oh!
            by the trumpet of Satchmo

plea smothered in the throat
of the lynched black

trickle of blood
sliding
along the powerful currents
            of the river
                Mississippi

Guy Tirolien

lent balancement
des corps
frénésie des sermons et longs cris d'hystérie
dans le roulis
    des églises noires
        du Missouri

éclairs verts jaillissant
    des bûchers crépitants
        de Virginie
          du Kentucky
            de Géorgie

désirs rouges réchauffant
    les nuits d'Alabama
        d'Oklahoma
          des Bahamas

non
ne fermez pas l'oreille
aux hoquets aux sanglots
aux subtils glissandos
à la stridence à l'insistance à la cadence
des blues
    — swingués oh!
        par la trompette de Satchmo

ne fermez pas l'oreille
aux rires aux soupirs
aux délires
aux éclats aux oua-oua
à la joie
qui se bousculent —
        ha ha!

slow swaying
of bodies
frenzy of sermons and long cries of hysteria
in the swell
    of black churches
        of Missouri

green lightning bursting
    from the crackling pyres
        of Virginia
          of Kentucky
            of Georgia

red desires warming
    the nights of Alabama
        of Oklahoma
          of the Bahamas

no
don't shut your ears
to the hiccups to the sobs
to the stridence to the insistence to the cadence
of the blues
    — swung oh!
        by the trumpet of Satchmo

don't shut your ears
to the laughter to the sighs
to the madness
to the peals to the wah-wah
to the joy
that collide —
        ha ha!

Guy Tirolien

qui s'accumulent —
                    j'te crois!
                        — dans la trompette de Satchmo

sourires des bébés noirs
éclairant la nuit
        noire
            d'Alabama
                d'Oklahoma
                    des Bahamas

joie truquée des filles noires
                    des filles jaunes
dans les cabarets noirs
                de Harlem
cherchant au fond d'un whisky brun
            d'un whisky or
le visage oublié
            d'un garçon brun
                d'un garçon jaune
                    de Bâton Rouge
                        ou de Natchez

rires du peuple noir
roulant dans les rues
            noires
            de Frisco
                de Chicago
                    de Santiago

that build —
              I believe 'ya!
                        — in the trumpet of Satchmo

smiles of black babies
lighting up the black
        night
        of Alabama
            of Oklahoma
                of the Bahamas

joy faked by black girls
            by yellow girls
in the black cabarets
                    of Harlem
looking in the bottom of a glass of brown whisky
            of gold whiskey for
the forgotten face
        of a brown boy
            of a yellow boy
                from Baton Rouge
                    or from Natchez

laughter of black people
rolling in the black
        streets
        of Frisco
            of Chicago
                of Santiago

Guy Tirolien

non
ne fermez pas l'oreille
aux rires aux soupirs
aux délires
aux éclats aux oua-oua
à la joie
qui se bousculent —
                ha ha!
qui s'accumulent —
                j'te crois!
                — dans la trompette de Satchmo

no
don't shut your ears
to the laughter to the sighs
to the madness
to the peals to the wah-wah
to the joy
that collide —

          ha ha!

that build —

          I believe 'ya!
             — in the trumpet of Satchmo

part two

Africa

Africa is the second largest continent after Asia, perhaps the birthplace of man, and the mother continent of Blacks all over the world. For centuries it was isolated, especially south of the Sahara Desert, by its formidable physical barriers. The violent disruptions caused by the slave trade were followed by colonial rule in the nineteenth and early twentieth centuries, but this phase has ended. The new republics saluted by Césaire in his poem to the Third World are developing their natural resources, expanding and strengthening their economies, and striving to educate their largely illiterate masses.

The poets in this section are from countries in Africa, and in one case, an island off its east coast, which were colonized by the French. French is not the native language of any African — over 400 other tribal languages are spoken on the continent — but in Senegal, the Ivory Coast, and the Congo French has remained as the language of international trade, diplomacy, and the educated elite. Many poets write in French to reach a larger audience; included here are three of the most important — Senghor, U'Tam'si, and Maunick — and three of the most accessible to American students — Dadié, Diakhaté, and Diop.

Léopold Sédar Senghor

SENGHOR AND THE POETS OF SENEGAL

Senegal, at Africa's westernmost tip, saw the birth of Léopold Sédar Senghor, the continent's leading exponent of Negritude, in 1906. He spent an idyllic childhood in a prosperous family of two dozen brothers and sisters, was educated in French missionary schools, and studied for the priesthood for four years only to be told that he had no religious vocation. Senghor's intellectual gifts were so outstanding that he was sent to Paris to study and became the first African to obtain the highest and most competitive French university degree. He taught in French schools and began to write. Like his co-founders of Negritude, Senghor pursued a political career after the war, first as a deputy from Senegal to the French Assembly, and then, in 1960, as the first president of the newly independent republic, a post he still held in 1971. His bonds to France are very strong, and some African nationalists accuse him of Francophilia. Few, however, fail to acknowledge that his stately, flowing poetry represents true African eloquence. Senghor's serene verse celebrates the splendors of the African people and land in rhythms inspired by the tom-tom and the melodies of the oral tradition in African poetry. David Diop and Lamine Diakhaté, also represented in this chapter, are but two of many Senegalese poets who might have been chosen. According to Senghor, "Poetry together with groundnuts is this country's greatest wealth."

Léopold Senghor

NUIT DE SINE

Femme, pose sur mon front tes mains balsamiques, tes mains
    douces plus que fourrure.
Là-haut les palmes balancées qui bruissent dans la haute brise
    nocturne
A peine. Pas même la chanson de nourrice.
Qu'il nous berce, le silence rythmé.
Écoutons son chant, écoutons battre notre sang sombre,
    écoutons
Battre le pouls profond de l'Afrique dans la brume des villages
    perdus.

Voici que décline la lune lasse vers son lit de mer étale
Voici que s'assoupissent les éclats de rire, que les conteurs
    eux-mêmes
Dodelinent de la tête comme l'enfant sur le dos de sa mère
Voici que les pieds des danseurs s'alourdissent, que s'alourdit
    la langue des choeurs alternés.

C'est l'heure des étoiles et de la Nuit qui songe
S'accoude à cette colline de nuages, drapée dans son long pagne
    de lait.
Les toits des cases luisent tendrement. Que disent-ils, si confi-
    dentiels, aux étoiles?
Dedans, le foyer s'éteint dans l'intimité d'odeurs âcres et douces.

Femme, allume la lampe au beurre clair, que causent autour les
    Ancêtres comme les parents, les enfants au lit.

NUIT DE SINE

Woman, lay on my forehead your perfumed hands, hands softer
     than fur.
Above, the swaying palm trees rustle in the high night breeze
Hardly at all. No lullaby even.
The rhythmic silence cradles us.
Listen to its song, listen to our dark blood beat, listen
To the deep pulse of Africa beating in the mist of forgotten
     villages.

See the tired moon comes down to her bed on the slack sea
The laughter grows weary, the story-tellers even
Are nodding their heads like a child on the back of its mother
The feet of the dancers grow heavy, and heavy the voice of the
     answering choirs.

It is the hour of stars, of Night that dreams
Leaning upon this hill of clouds, wrapped in its long milky cloth.
The roofs of the huts gleam tenderly. What do they say so
     secretly to the stars?
Inside the fire goes out among intimate smells that are acrid
     and sweet.

Woman, light the clear oil lamp, where the ancestors gathered
     around may talk as parents talk when the children are put
     to bed.

Léopold Senghor

Écoutons la voix des Anciens d'Elissa. Comme nous exilés
Ils n'ont pas voulu mourir, que se perdît par les sables leur tor-
rent séminal.
Que j'écoute, dans la case enfumée que visite un reflet d'âmes
propices
Ma tête sur ton sein chaud comme un dang au sortir du feu
et fumant
Que je respire l'odeur de nos Morts, que je recueille et redise
leur voix vivante, que j'apprenne à
Vivre avant de descendre, au-delà du plongeur, dans les hautes
profondeurs du sommeil.

JARDIN DE FRANCE

Calme jardin,
Grave jardin,
Jardin aux yeux baissés au soir
Pour la nuit,
Peines et rumeurs,
Toutes les angoisses bruissantes de la Ville
Arrivent jusqu'à moi, glissant sur les toits lisses,
Arrivent à la fenêtre
Penchée, tamisées par feuilles menues et tendres et pensives.

Mains blanches,
Gestes délicats,
Gestes apaisants.

Listen to the voice of the ancients of Elissa[1]. Exiled like us

They have never wanted to die, to let the torrent of their seed
be lost in the sands.

Let me listen in the smoky hut where there comes a glimpse of
the friendly spirits

My head on your bosom warm like a *dang*[2] still steaming from
the fire.

Let me breathe the smell of our Dead, gather and speak out
again their living voice, learn to

Live before I go down, deeper than diver, into the high pro-
fundities of sleep.

GARDEN OF FRANCE

Calm garden,
Grave garden,
Garden with eyes lowered in the evening
For the night,
Troubles and rumors,
All the rustling anguish of the City
Reaches me, sliding down the smooth roofs
Arriving at the window
Bent, sifted by leaves slight and tender and pensive.

White hands
Delicate gestures
Placating gestures

[1]Village in upper Portuguese Guinea from which Senghor's family originates.
[2]Wolof word for an African dish of granulated flour, steamed over broth,
frequently with meat added.

Mais l'appel du tam-tam
               bondissant
                        par monts
                              et
                                    continents,
Qui l'apaisera, mon coeur,
A l'appel du tam-tam
               bondissant,
                        véhément,
                                lancinant?

FEMME NOIRE

Femme nue, femme noire
Vêtue de ta couleur qui est vie, de ta forme qui est beauté!
J'ai grandi à ton ombre; la douceur de tes mains bandait mes
    yeux.
Et voilà qu'au coeur de l'Été et de Midi, je te découvre, Terre
    promise, du haut d'un haut col calciné
Et ta beauté me foudroie en plein coeur, comme l'éclair d'un
    aigle.

Femme nue, femme obscure
Fruit mûr à la chair ferme, sombres extases du vin noir, bouche
    qui fais lyrique ma bouche
Savane aux horizons purs, savane qui frémis aux caresses fer-
    ventes du Vent d'Est
Tamtam sculpté, tamtam tendu qui grondes sous les doigts du
    vainqueur
Ta voix grave de contralto est le chant spirituel de l'Aimée.

But the call of the tom-tom
> bounding
>> across mountains
>> and
>>> continents,

Who will placate my heart
At the call of the tom-tom
> bounding
>> vehement
>>> throbbing?

BLACK WOMAN

Naked woman, black woman
Clothed with your colour which is life, with your form which
    is beauty!
In your shadow I have grown up; the gentleness of your hands
    was laid over my eyes.
And now, high up on the sun-baked pass, at the heart of summer,
    at the heart of noon, I come upon you, my Promised Land,
And your beauty strikes me to the heart like the flash of an eagle.

Naked woman, dark woman
Firm-fleshed ripe fruit, sombre raptures of black wine, mouth
    making lyrical my mouth
Savannah stretching to clear horizons, savannah shuddering
    beneath the East Wind's eager caresses
Carved tom-tom, taut tom-tom, muttering under the Con-
    queror's fingers
Your solemn contralto voice is the spiritual song of the Beloved.

Femme nue, femme obscure
Huile que ne ride nul souffle, huile calme aux flancs de l'athlète,
    aux flancs des princes du Mali
Gazelle aux attaches célestes, les perles sont étoiles sur la nuit
    de ta peau
Délices des jeux de l'esprit, les reflets de l'or rouge sur ta peau
    qui se moire
A l'ombre de ta chevelure, s'éclaire mon angoisse aux soleils
    prochains de tes yeux.

Femme nue, femme noire
Je chante ta beauté qui passe, forme que je fixe dans l'Éternel
Avant que le Destin jaloux ne te réduise en cendres pour nourrir
    les racines de la vie.

AUX TIRAILLEURS SÉNÉGALAIS
MORTS POUR LA FRANCE

Voici le Soleil
Qui fait tendre la poitrine des vierges
Qui fait sourire sur les bancs verts les vieillards
Qui réveillerait les morts sous une terre maternelle.
J'entends le bruit des canons — est-ce d'Irun?
On fleurit les tombes, on réchauffe le Soldat Inconnu.
Vous mes frères obscurs, personne ne vous nomme.
On promet cinq mille de vos enfants à la gloire des futurs morts,
    on les remercie d'avance futurs morts obscurs

Naked woman, dark woman
Oil that no breath ruffles, calm oil on the athlete's flanks, on the
    flanks of the Princes of Mali
Gazelle limbed in Paradise, pearls are stars on the night of your
    skin
Delights of the mind, the glinting of red gold against your
    watered skin
Under the shadow of your hair, my care is lightened by the
    neighbouring suns of your eyes.

Naked woman, black woman,
I sing your beauty that passes, the form that I fix in the Eternal,
Before jealous Fate turn you to ashes to feed the roots of life.

TO THE SENEGALESE SHARPSHOOTERS
DEAD FOR FRANCE

Here is the Sun
That makes virgins' breasts bold
That makes old people on green benches smile
That would wake the dead under a maternal earth
I hear the noise of cannon — is it from Irun?[1]
They're putting flowers on graves and warming up the Unknown
    Soldier.
You my dark brothers, no one names you.
They promise five hundred thousand of your children to the
    glory of the future dead, thanked in advance the future dark
    dead

[1]City in Spain, a scene of action during the Spanish Civil War.

Léopold Senghor

Die Schwarze schande!

Écoutez-moi, Tirailleurs sénégalais, dans la solitude de la terre
noire et de la mort
Dans votre solitude sans yeux sans oreilles, plus que dans ma
peau sombre au fond de la Province
Sans même la chaleur de vos camarades couchés tout contre
vous, comme jadis dans la tranchée jadis dans les palabres
du village
Écoutez-moi, Tirailleurs à la peau noire, bien que sans oreilles
et sans yeux dans votre triple enceinte de nuit.

Nous n'avons pas loué de pleureuses, pas même les larmes de
vos femmes anciennes
— Elles ne se rappellent que vos grands coups de colère, préfé-
rant l'ardeur des vivants.
Les plaintes des pleureuses trop claires
Trop vite asséchées les joues de vos femmes, comme en saison
sèche les torrents du Fouta
Les larmes les plus chaudes trop claires et trop vite bues au coin
des lèvres oublieuses.
Nous vous apportons, écoutez-nous qui épelions vos noms dans
les mois que vous mouriez
Nous, dans ces jours de peur sans mémoire, vous apportons
l'amitié de vos camarades d'âge.
Ah! puissé-je un jour d'une voix couleur de braise, puissé-je
chanter
L'amitié des camarades fervente comme des entrailles et
délicate, forte comme des tendons.
Écoutez-nous, Morts étendus dans l'eau au profond des plaines
du Nord et de l'Est.

Léopold Senghor

Die Schwarze schande![1]

Listen to me Senegalese Sharpshooters, in the loneliness of black
    earth and death
In your eyeless earless loneliness, more than in my somber skin
    in the heart of the country
Without even the warmth of your comrades lying against you as
    once in the trench once in village palavers
Listen to me, Sharpshooters with black skin, even though earless
    and eyeless in your triple enclosure of night.

We have not rented mourners, not even the tears of your former
    wives
— They remember only your great flashes of anger, preferring
    the ardor of the living.
The laments of mourners are too light
Too quickly dried the cheeks of your wives, like the Fouta water-
    falls in dry season
The warmest tears too clear and too quickly drunk in the corners
    of forgetful mouths.

We bring you, listen to us, we who would spell your names
    in the months when you were dying
We, in these days of fear without memory, bring you the friend-
    ship of your peer companions.
Ah! that I might one day with a voice the color of glowing
    embers, that I might sing
The friendship of comrades fervent as entrails and delicate,
    strong as tendons.
Listen to us, Dead stretched out in the water of the depths of the
    Northern and Eastern plains.

---

[1]"Black disgrace," the expression is used in German to describe an unspeak-
able abomination, *viz.* "black hole of Calcutta" in English.

Recevez ce sol rouge, sous le soleil d'été ce sol rougi du sang
    des blanches hosties
Recevez le salut de vos camarades noirs, Tirailleurs sénégalais
MORTS POUR LA RÉPUBLIQUE!

Tours 1938.

AUX SOLDATS NÉGRO-AMÉRICAINS

À Mercer Cook

Je ne vous ai pas reconnus sous votre prison d'uniformes couleur
    de tristesse
Je ne vous ai pas reconnus sous la calebasse du casque sans
    panache
Je n'ai pas reconnu le hennissement chevrotant de vos chevaux
    de fer, qui boivent mais ne mangent pas.
Et ce n'est plus la noblesse des éléphants, c'est la lourdeur
    barbare des monstres des prétemps du monde.
Sous votre visage fermé, je ne vous ai pas reconnus.
J'ai touché seulement la chaleur de votre main brune, je me suis
    nommé: «Afrika!»
Et j'ai retrouvé le rire perdu, j'ai salué la voix ancienne et le
    grondement des cascades du Congo.
Frères, je ne sais si c'est vous qui avez bombardé les cathédrales,
    orgueil de l'Europe
Si vous êtes la foudre dont la main de Dieu a brûlé Sodome et
    Gomorrhe.
Non, vous êtes les messagers de sa merci, le souffle du Printemps
    après l'Hiver.

Receive this red soil, under the summer sun this soil red from the
blood of white victims

Receive the salute of your black comrades, Senegalese Sharp-
shooters

DEAD FOR THE REPUBLIC!

Tours 1938

TO THE AMERICAN NEGRO SOLDIERS

To Mercer Cook

I did not recognize you in your prison of sad-coloured uniforms

I did not recognize you under that calabash helmet with no
plume

I did not recognize the quavering whinny of your iron horses
that drink but do not eat.

No longer the nobility of elephants but the barbaric clumsiness
of monsters from the foretime of the world.

Under your closed faces I did not recognize you.

I only touched the warmth of your brown hand. I said my name,
'Afrika!'

And found again lost laughter, I greeted the ancient voice and
the roar of the cascades of the Congo.

Brothers, I do not know if it was you who bombed the cathe-
drals, the pride of Europe

If you are the lightning that in God's hand burnt Sodom and
Gomorrah.

No, you are the messengers of his mercy, breath of Spring after
Winter.

A ceux qui avaient oublié le rire — ils ne se servaient plus que
　　d'une sourire oblique
Qui ne connaissaient plus que la saveur salée des larmes et
　　l'irritante odeur du sang
Vous apportez le printemps de la Paix et l'espoir au bout de
　　l'attente.
Et leur nuit se remplit d'une douceur de lait, les champs bleus du
　　ciel se couvrent de fleurs, le silence chante suavement.
Vous leur apportez le soleil. L'air palpite de murmures liquides
　　et de pépiements cristallins et de battements soyeux d'ailes
Les cités aériennes sont tièdes de nids.
Par les rues de joie ruisselante, les garçons jouent avec leurs
　　rêves
Les hommes dansent devant leurs machines et se surprennent à
　　chanter.
Les paupières des écolières sont pétales de roses, les fruits
　　mûrissent à la poitrine des vierges
Et les hanches des femmes — oh! douceur — généreusement
　　s'alourdissent.
Frères noirs, guerriers dont la bouche est fleur qui chante
— Oh! délice de vivre après l'Hiver — je vous salue comme des
　　messagers de paix.

À NEW YORK

(pour un orchestre de jazz: solo de trompette)

I

New York! D'abord j'ai été confondu par ta beauté, ces grandes
filles d'or aux jambes longues.

For those who had forgotten laughter (using only an oblique smile)

Who had forgotten the salt taste of tears and the irritant smell of blood

You bring the springtime of Peace, hope at the end of waiting.

And their night fills with a sweetness of milk, the blue fields of the sky are covered with flowers, softly the silence sings.

You bring the sun. The air throbs with liquid murmurs and crystalline whistling and the silky beat of wings

Aerial cities are warm with nests.

Down streets running with joy, boys play with their dreams

Men dance before their machines, and catch themselves singing.

The eyelids of schoolgirls are rose petals, fruits ripen at the breasts of virgins

The hips of the women — O sweetness — grow full and heavy.

Black brothers, warriors whose mouths are singing flowers

— O delight to live after Winter — I greet you as the messengers of peace.

NEW YORK

Jazz orchestra: solo trumpet

I

New York! At first your beauty confused me, and your great long-legged golden girls.

Si timide d'abord devant tes yeux de métal bleu, ton sourire de
　　givre
Si timide. Et l'angoisse au fond des rues à gratte-ciel
Levant des yeux de chouette parmi l'éclipse du soleil.
Sulfureuse ta lumière et les fûts livides, dont les têtes foudroient
　　le ciel
Les gratte-ciel qui défient les cyclones sur leurs muscles d'acier
　　et leur peau patinée de pierres.
Mais quinze jours sur les trottoirs chauves de Manhattan
— C'est au bout de la troisième semaine que vous saisit la fièvre
　　en un bond de jaguar
Quinze jours sans un puits ni pâturage, tous les oiseaux de l'air
Tombant soudain et morts sous les hautes cendres des terrasses.
Pas un rire d'enfant en fleur, sa main dans ma main fraîche
Pas un sein maternel, des jambes de nylon. Des jambes et des
　　seins sans sueur ni odeur.
Pas un mot tendre en l'absence de lèvres, rien que des coeurs
　　artificiels payés en monnaie forte
Et pas un livre où lire la sagesse. La palette du peintre fleurit des
　　cristaux de corail.
Nuits d'insomnie ô nuits de Manhattan! si agitées de feux follets,
　　tandis que les klaxons hurlent des heures vides
Et que les eaux obscures charrient des amours hygiéniques, tels
　　des fleuves en crue des cadavres d'enfants.

II

Voici le temps des signes et des comptes
New York! or voici le temps de la manne et de l'hysope.
Il n'est que d'écouter les trombones de Dieu, ton coeur battre
　　au rythme du sang ton sang.
J'ai vu dans Harlem bourdonnant de bruits de couleurs solen-
　　nelles et d'odeurs flamboyantes

I was so timid at first under your blue metallic eyes, your frosty
    smile
So timid. And the disquiet in the depth of your skyscraper streets
Lifting up owl eyes in the sun's eclipse.
Your sulphurous light and the livid shafts (their heads dumb-
    founding the sky)
Skyscrapers defying cyclones on their muscles of steel and their
    weathered stone skins.
But a fortnight on the bald sidewalks of Manhattan
— At the end of the third week the fever takes you with the
    pounce of a jaguar
A fortnight with no well or pasture, all the birds of the air
Fall suddenly dead below the high ashes of the terraces.
No child's laughter blossoms, his hand in my fresh hand
No mother's breast. Legs in nylon. Legs and breasts with no
    sweat and no smell.
No tender word for mouths are lipless. Hard cash buys artificial
    hearts.
No book where wisdom is read. The painter's palette flowers
    with crystals of coral.
Insomniac nights O nights of Manhattan, tormented by fatuous
    fires, while the klaxons cry through the empty hours
And dark waters bear away hygienic loves, like the bodies of
    children on a river in flood.

II

It is the time of signs and reckonings
New York! It is the time of manna and hyssop.
Only listen to God's trombones, your heart beating to the
    rhythm of blood your blood.
I have seen Harlem humming with sounds and solemn colour
    and flamboyant smells

— C'est l'heure du thé chez le livreur-en-produits-pharma-
ceutiques

J'ai vu se préparer la fête de la Nuit à la fuite du jour. Je proclame
la Nuit plus véridique que le jour.

C'est l'heure pure où dans les rues, Dieu fait germer la vie
d'avant mémoire

Tous les éléments amphibies rayonnants comme des soleils.

Harlem Harlem! voici ce que j'ai vu Harlem Harlem! Une brise
verte de blés sourdre des pavés labourés par les pieds nus
de danseurs Dans

Croupes ondes de soie et seins de fers de lance, ballets de
nénuphars et de masques fabuleux

Aux pieds des chevaux de police, les mangues de l'amour rouler
des maisons basses.

Et j'ai vu le long des trottoirs, des ruisseaux de rhum blanc des
ruisseaux de lait noir dans le brouillard bleu des cigares.

J'ai vu le ciel neiger au soir des fleurs de coton et des ailes de
séraphins et des panaches de sorciers.

Écoute New York! ô écoute ta voix mâle de cuivre ta voix
vibrante de hautbois, l'angoisse bouchée de tes larmes
tomber en gros caillots de sang

Écoute au loin battre ton coeur nocturne, rythme et sang du
tam-tam, tam-tam sang et tam-tam.

III

New York! je dis New York, laisse affluer le sang noir dans ton
sang

Qu'il dérouille tes articulations d'acier, comme une huile de vie

Qu'il donne à tes ponts la courbe des croupes et la souplesse des
lianes.

Voici revenir les temps très anciens, l'unité retrouvée la récon-
ciliation du Lion du Taureau et de l'Arbre

—(It is tea-time for the man who delivers pharmaceutical products)

I have seen them preparing at flight of day, the festival of the Night. I proclaim there is more truth in the Night than in the day.

It is the pure hour when God sets the life before memory germinating in the streets

All the amphibious elements shining like suns.

Harlem Harlem! I have seen Harlem Harlem! A breeze green with corn springing from the pavements ploughed by the bare feet of dancers In

Crests and waves of silk and breasts of spearheads, ballets of lilies and fabulous masks

The mangoes of love roll from the low houses under the police horses' hooves.

I have seen down the sidewalks streams of white rum and streams of black milk in the blue haze of cigars.

I have seen the sky at evening snowing cotton flowers and wings of seraphim and wizard's plumes.

Listen, New York, listen to your brazen male voice your vibrant oboe voice, the muted anguish of your tears falling in great clots of blood

Listen to the far beating of your nocturnal heart, rhythm and blood of the drum, drum and blood and drum.

III

New York! I say to New York, let the black blood flow into your blood

Cleaning the rust from your steel articulations, like an oil of life

Giving your bridges the curve of the hills, the liana's suppleness.

See, the ancient times come again, unity is rediscovered the reconciliation of the Lion the Bull and the Tree

L'idée liée à l'acte l'oreille au coeur le signe au sens.
Voilà tes fleuves bruissants de caïmans musqués et de lamantins
    aux yeux de mirages. Et nul besoin d'inventer les Sirènes.
Mais il suffit d'ouvrir les yeux à l'arc-en-ciel d'Avril
Et les oreilles, surtout les oreilles à Dieu qui d'une rire de saxo-
    phone créa le ciel et la terre en six jours.
Et le septième jour, il dormit du grand sommeil nègre.

ÉLÉGIE DES CIRCONCIS

Nuit d'enfance, Nuit bleue Nuit blonde ô Lune!
Combien de fois t'ai-je invoquée ô Nuit! pleurant au bord des
    routes
Au bord des douleurs de mon âge d'homme? Solitude! et c'est
    les dunes alentour.
Or c'était nuit d'enfance extrême, dense comme la poix.
La peur courbait les dos sous les rugissements des lions
Courbait les hautes herbes le silence sournois de cette nuit.
Feu de branches toi feu d'espoir! pâle mémoire du Soleil qui
    rassurait mon innocence
A peine — il me fallait mourir. Je portais la main à mon cou,
    comme la vierge qui frissonne à l'horreur de la mort.
Il me fallait mourir à la beauté du chant — toutes choses
    dérivent au fil de la mort.
Voyez le crépuscule à la gorge de tourterelle, quand roucoulent
    bleues les palombes
Et volent les mouettes du rêve avec des cris plaintifs.

The idea is linked to the act the ear to the heart the sign to the
sense.
See your rivers murmuring with musky caymans, manatees with
eyes of mirage. There is no need to invent the Mermaids.
It is enough to open your eyes to the April rainbow
And the ears, above all the ears to God who with a burst of
saxophone laughter created the heavens and the earth in
six days.
And on the seventh day, he slept his great negro sleep.

ELEGY OF THE CIRCUMCISED

Night of childhood, blue Night, blond Night O Moon!
How often have I called to you, Night, crying by the roadside
By the side of the sorrows of my manhood? Solitude — and all
about us are the dunes.
It was night of earliest childhood, thick as pitch. Fear bowed our
backs under the Lion's roaring.
Tall grasses bowed under the shifty silence of that night.
Fire of branches you fire of hope! Pale memory of the Sun,
heartening my innocence
Hardly at all. I had to die. I laid my hand on my throat like a girl
who shudders at the horror of Death
I had to die to the beauty of song — all things drift with the
current of Death.
See the twilight on the throat of the dove when blue pigeons call
And the seamews of dream fly with plaintive cries.

Léopold Senghor

Mourons et dansons coude à coude en une guirlande tressée

Que la robe n'emprisonne nos pas, mais rutile le don de la promise, éclairs sous les nuages.

Le tam-tam laboure *woi!* le silence sacré. Dansons, le chant fouette le sang

Le rythme chasse cette angoisse qui nous tient à la gorge.

La vie tient la mort à distance.

Dansons au refrain de l'angoisse, que se lève la nuit du sexe dessus notre ignorance dessus notre innocence.

Ah! mourir à l'enfance, que meure le poème se désintègre la syntaxe, que s'abîment tous les mots qui ne sont pas essentiels.

Le poids du rythme suffit, pas besoin de mots-ciment pour bâtir sur le roc la cité de demain.

Surgisse le Soleil de la mer des ténèbres

Sang! Les flots sont couleur d'aurore.

Mais Dieu, tant de fois ai-je lamenté — combien de fois? — les nuits d'enfance transparentes.

Midi-le-Mâle est l'heure des Esprits, où toute forme se dépouille de sa chair

Comme les arbres en Europe sous le soleil d'hiver.

Voilà, les os sont abstraits, ils ne se prêtent qu'aux calculs de la règle du compas du sextant.

La vie comme le sable s'échappe aux doigts de l'homme, les cristaux de neige emprisonnent la vie de l'eau

Le serpent de l'eau glisse aux mains vaines des roseaux.

Nuits chères Nuits amies, et Nuits d'enfance, parmi les tanns parmi les bois

Nuits palpitantes de présences, et de paupières, si peuplées d'ailes et de souffles

Let us die, let us dance, elbow to elbow woven together like a
  garland
No dress to hinder our steps, but the gift of the promise glows,
  lightning under the clouds.
Woi! the drum ploughs up the holy silence. Dance. Song lashes
  the blood
Rhythm drives out the fear that has us by the throat. Life holds
  death at bay.
Dance to the burthen of fear, that the night of the phallus may
  rise over our ignorance over our innocence.
Ah! die to childhood, let the poem die the syntax fall apart, let
  all the inessential words be swallowed up.
The weight of the rhythm is enough, no need of word-cement to
  build on the rock the City of tomorrow.
Let the sun rise from the sea of shadows
Blood! The waves are the colour of dawn.

But God, so many times I have wept — how many times? — for
  the transparent nights of childhood.
Midday the Male is the hour of Spirits when every form strips
  off its flesh
Like the trees in Europe under the winter sun.
See, the bones are abstract, lending themselves only to calcula-
  tions with straight edge, compass and sextant.
Life runs through the fingers of man like sand, crystals of snow
  imprison the life of the water
The serpent of water slips through the helpless hands of the
  reeds.
Dear Nights friendly Nights, Nights of Childhood, among the
  seaflats among the woods
Nights quivering with presences, brushed with eyelids, peopled
  with wings and sounds of breathing

De silence vivant, dites combien de fois vous ai-je lamentées au
   mitan de mon âge?

Le poème se fane au soleil de midi, il se nourrit de la rosée du
   soir
Et rythme le tam-tam le battement de la sève sous le parfum des
   fruits mûrs.
Maître des Initiés, j'ai besoin je le sais de ton savoir pour percer
   le chiffre des choses
Prendre connaissance de mes fonctions de père et de lamarque
Mesurer exactement le champ de mes charges, répartir la
   moisson sans oublier un ouvrier ni orphelin.
Le chant n'est pas que charme, il nourrit les têtes laineuses de
   mon troupeau.
Le poème est oiseau-serpent, les noces de l'ombre et de la
   lumière à l'aube
Il monte Phénix! il chante les ailes déployées, sur le carnage des
   paroles.

LE TOTEM

Il me faut le cacher au plus intime de mes veines
L'Ancêtre à la peau d'orage sillonée d'éclairs et de foudre
Mon animal gardien, il me faut le cacher
Que je ne rompe le barrage des scandales.
Il est mon sang fidèle qui requiert fidélité
Protégeant mon orgueil nu contre
Moi-même et la superbe des races heureuses...

And with breathing silence, say how many times have I sorrowed
  for you in the noontime of my age?

The poem droops in the sun of Noon, it feeds on the dew of
  evening
And the drum beats out the rhythm of the sap under the smell of
  ripened fruits.
Master of the Initiates, I know I need your wisdom to break the
  cypher of things
To learn my office as father, as lamarch[1]
To measure exactly the field of my duties, to share out the
  harvest forgetting neither worker nor orphan.
The song is not only a charm, by it the woolly heads of my flock
  are fed.
The poem is bird-serpent, marriage of shadow and dawnlight
The Phoenix rises, he sings with wings extended, over the
  carnage of words.

TOTEM

I must hide in the intimate depths of my veins
The Ancestor storm-dark skinned, shot with lightning and
  thunder
And my guardian animal, I must hide him
Lest I smash through the boom of scandal.
He is my faithful blood and demands fidelity
Protecting my naked pride against
Myself and all the insolence of lucky races. . .

---

[1]Word formed by Senghor from the Serer word *lan,* meaning land, and the
Greek *archos,* commander; therefore, landowner.

David Diop

VAGUES

Les vagues furieuses de la liberté
Claquent sur la Bête affolée
de l'esclave d'hier un combattant est né
Et le docker de Suez et le coolie d'Hanoï
Tous ceux qu'on intoxique de fatalité
Lancent leur chant immense au milieu des vagues
Les vagues furieuses de la liberté
Qui claquent sur la Bête affolée.

AFRIQUE

À ma mère

Afrique mon Afrique
Afrique des fiers guerriers dans les savanes ancestrales
Afrique que chante ma grand-mère
Au bord de son fleuve lointain
Je ne t'ai jamais connue
Mais mon regard est plein de ton sang
Ton beau sang noir à travers les champs répandu
Le sang de ta sueur
La sueur de ton travail

David Diop was killed in a plane crash in 1960 at the age of 33. Brought to France when he was eight, and there a student of Senghor's, the talented Senegalese took part in the post-war *Présence Africaine* cultural movement headed by his uncle Alioune Diop. He was teaching school in newly independent Guinea when he died.

WAVES

The furious waves of liberty
Slap against the maddened Beast
from yesterday's slave a fighter is born
And the Suez docker and the Hanoi coolie
All those intoxicated by fatality
Launch their immense chant in the middle of the waves
The furious waves of liberty
That slap against the maddened Beast.

AFRICA

To my mother

Africa my Africa
Africa of proud warriors in the ancestral savannahs
Africa that my grandmother sings
On her distant river banks
I have never known you
But my glance is full of your blood
Your beautiful black blood spilt over the fields
The blood of your sweat
The sweat of your work

Le travail de l'esclavage
L'esclavage de tes enfants
Afrique dis-moi Afrique
Est-ce donc toi ce dos qui se courbe
Et se couche sous le poids de l'humilité
Ce dos tremblant à zébrures rouges
Qui dit oui au fouet sur la route de Midi
Alors gravement une voix me répondit
Fils impétueux cet arbre robuste et jeune
Cet arbre là-bas
Splendidement seul au milieu des fleurs blanches et fanées
C'est l'Afrique ton Afrique qui repousse
Qui repousse patiemment obstinément
Et dont les fruits ont peu à peu
L'amère saveur de la liberté.

À UNE DANSEUSE NOIRE

Négresse ma chaude rumeur d'Afrique
Ma terre d'énigme et mon fruit de raison
Tu es danse par la joie nue de ton sourire
Par l'offrande de tes seins et tes secrets pouvoirs
Tu es danse par les légendes d'or des nuits nuptiales
Par les temps nouveaux et les rythmes séculaires
Négresse triomphe multiplié de rêves et d'étoiles
Maîtresse docile à l'étreinte des koras
Tu es danse par le vertige
Par la magie des reins recommençant le monde
Tu es danse

The work of your slavery
The slavery of your children
Africa tell me Africa
Can this be really you this back that bends
And lies down under the weight of humility
This trembling red-striped back
That says yes to the whip on the Noon road
Then gravely a voice answers me
Impetuous son that robust young tree
That tree there
Splendidly alone among the faded white flowers
That is Africa your Africa growing again
Growing again patiently stubbornly
And its fruits take on little by little
The bitter taste of freedom.

TO A BLACK DANCER

Negress my warm sound of Africa
My land of enigma and my fruit of reason
You are the dance through the naked joy of your smile
Through the offering of your breasts and your secret powers
You are dance through the golden legends of nuptial nights
Through new times and age-old rhythms
Negress triumph multiplied by dreams and stars
Mistress docile to the kora's[1] embrace
You are dance through dizziness
Through the magic of loins beginning the world again
You are dance

[1]African stringed instrument resembling a harp.

Et les mythes autour de moi brûlent
Autour de moi les perruques du savoir
En grands feux de joie dans le ciel de tes pas
Tu es danse
Et brûlent les faux dieux sous ta flamme verticale
Tu es le visage de l'initié
Sacrifiant la folie auprès de l'arbre-gardien
Tu es l'idée du Tout et la voix de l'Ancien.
Lancée grave à l'assaut des chimères
Tu es le Verbe qui explose
En gerbes miraculeuses sur les côtes de l'oubli.

Lamine Diakhaté

SUR LE TOMBEAU DE JOHN KENNEDY (fragment)

Ceux-là qui reculèrent la forêt au rythme
de leurs doigts
ils plièrent la vie à leur volonté de survivre
Ils étaient là attentifs en l'An 60
du chiffre des choses
lorsque tu surgis étoile de vie sur leur espoir de vivre
Ils t'acclamèrent au son des blues
te dirent leur passion
Ta tête leur devint panache

And the myths around me burn
Around me the wigs of learning
In great fires of joy in the heaven of your steps
You are dance
And the false gods burn under your vertical flame
You are the face of the initiated
Sacrificing folly alongside the guardian tree
You are the idea of Everything and the voice of the Ancient
Grave catapult assaulting chimera
You are the Word that explodes
In miraculous fireworks on the slopes of forgetfulness.

Lamine Diakhaté, a contemporary of Diop, has pursued his
poetic career while serving in the Senghor government and
participating in African cultural affairs. The following
excerpt from a longer poem, which like many of his poems
is topical, suggests how John F. Kennedy was regarded at
his death by Third World intellectuals.

FOR JOHN KENNEDY'S TOMBSTONE (excerpt)

Those who pushed back the forest in rhythm
with their fingers
bent life to their will to survive
They were there attentive in the Year 60
to the sign of things
when you came forth a star of life over their hope to live
They acclaimed you to the sound of the blues
told you of their passion
Your head became their standard

Ils retrouvèrent le chemin du rêve
Leur rêve de fraternité
leur identité au coin du soleil de la Paix
Tu es allé à eux, sans escorte, sans méfiance
tes mains pures
Leurs visages sous la brise de la confiance redécouverte
Les têtes émergèrent
les regards de soleil les muscles libérés
la parole sans entrave à travers syllabes épurées
Tu leur parlas le langage antique des Pionniers
Ils sentirent les accents de l'Ancien Testament
eux si religieux
En toi ils revirent Abraham LINCOLN
Ils entendirent Walt WHITMAN le pionnier
Tu étais leur pionnier
Tu étais leur chiffre, leur totem en cette année 60
du chiffre des choses
Ils t'appelèrent JACK

They found the road of dreams again
Their dreams of fraternity
their identity in the sunny corner of Peace
You went to them unescorted unwary
your hands pure
Their faces swept by rediscovered trust
Their heads emerged
their glances sunny their muscles freed
in your unfettered speech of crisp syllables
You spoke to them in the ancient language of the Pioneers
They felt the Old Testament accents
they so religious
In you they saw Abraham LINCOLN again
They heard Walt WHITMAN the pioneer
You were their pioneer
You were their sign, their totem in that year 60
of the sign of things
They called you JACK

Bernard Dadié

BERNARD DADIÉ OF THE IVORY COAST

Dadié's homeland, the Ivory Coast, is located on the coast of West Africa, south of Mali. This poet is perhaps best known for his autobiographical novels *Climbié* and *A Negro in Paris* and for his collection of African tales and legends, which reflect his abiding interest in African art and folklore. Born in 1916 in the seaboard forest country of Assinie, Dadié began working on a plantation with a book-loving uncle when he was six. He supplemented his formal schooling with a year of self-tutoring, and was finally sent to normal school in Senegal. After 12 years in the Senegalese bureaucracy he became Inspector General of Education.

Following World War II, Dadié returned to the Ivory Coast and worked for a newspaper, where his anti-colonial stance landed him in a French prison. Upon his release, he continued to write articles, without signing them. When the Ivory Coast became independent from France in 1960, Dadié became Minister of Information; since 1963, he has been Director of Fine Arts and Research. Once the poet of the oppressed, he is now the poet of reconciliation. His direct poetry is considered over-simplistic by some, but it is so characteristic of the loving, universal spirit of African humanism that it merits attention.

Bernard Dadié

JE VOUS REMERCIE MON DIEU

Je vous remercie mon Dieu, de m'avoir créé Noir,
d'avoir fait de moi
la somme de toutes les douleurs,
mis sur ma tête,
le Monde.
J'ai la livrée du Centaure
Et je porte le Monde depuis le premier matin.

Le blanc est une couleur de circonstance
Le noir, la couleur de tous les jours
Et je porte le Monde depuis le premier soir.

Je suis content
de la forme de ma tête
faite pour porter le Monde,
Satisfait
de la forme de mon nez
Qui doit humer tout le vent du Monde,
Heureux
de la forme de mes jambes
Prêtes à courir toutes les étapes du Monde.

Je vous remercie mon Dieu, de m'avoir créé Noir,
d'avoir fait de moi,
la somme de toutes les douleurs.

Trente-six épées ont transpercé mon coeur.
Trente-six brasiers ont brûlé mon corps.
Et mon sang sur tous les calvaires a rougi la neige,
Et mon sang à tous les levants a rougi la nature.

Bernard Dadié

I THANK YOU GOD

I thank you God for having created me Black,
for having made of me
the sum of all sorrows,
put on my head,
the World.
I wear the Centaur's uniform
And I've been carrying the World since the first morning.

White is a color for occasions
Black the color of every day
And I've been carrying the World since the first evening.

I am content
with the shape of my head
made to carry the World,
Satisfied
with the shape of my nose
That must inhale all the wind in the World,
Happy
with the shape of my legs
Ready to run all the relays in the World.

I thank you God for having created me Black,
for having made of me,
the sum of all sorrows.

Thirty-six swords have pierced my heart.
Thirty-six braziers have seared my body.
And my blood has reddened the snow on every calvary,
And my blood has reddened nature at every sunrise.

Je suis quand même
Content de porter le Monde,
Content de mes bras courts
    de mes bras longs
      de l'épaisseur de mes lèvres.

Je vous remercie mon Dieu, de m'avoir créé Noir,
Je porte le Monde depuis l'aube des temps
Et mon rire sur le Monde,
    dans la nuit
      crée le jour.

CE QUE M'A DONNÉ LA FRANCE

La France ne m'a donné ni le fusil, ni la poudre, ni les balles qui couchent à jamais des frères Noirs ou Blancs.

Elle ne m'a donné ni mes menottes, ni mes années de prison, ni la misère dont je suis accablé.

Elle ne m'a donné ni mon taudis, ni mes guenilles, ni le code d'iniquité, ni la fosse commune.

Par contre elle m'a donné en exemple Vercingétorix disputant avec rage, la Gaule à César.

Elle m'a montré Voltaire, Balzac, Hugo, Peri, Danielle, tous les héros qui éclairent sa route de gloire, tous les écrivains et ces braves gens qui traitent l'homme en frère.

I am all the same
Content to carry the World,
Content with my short arms
        with my long arms
                with the thickness of my lips.

I thank you God for having created me Black,
I have been carrying the World since the dawn of time
And my laughter over the World,
        in the night
                creates the day.

WHAT FRANCE HAS GIVEN ME

France hasn't given me the rifle nor the powder nor the bullets which fell forever Black and White brothers.

She hasn't given me my handcuffs, nor my years of prison, nor the misery which overwhelms me.

She hasn't given me my slum, nor my rags, nor the code of iniquity, nor the common grave.

But she has given me the example of Vercingétorix[1] disputing furiously with Caesar for Gaul.

She showed me Voltaire, Balzac, Hugo, Peri,[2] Danielle, all the heroes who brighten her road to glory, all the writers and the good people who treat man like a brother.

[1]Leader of the Gauls who fought Caesar's invasion.
[2]Gabrielle Peri (1902-1941), journalist, politician, and head of the French Communist Resistance in World War II, was shot by the Nazis in 1941.

Bernard Dadié

Elle m'a montré Pasteur et la pléiade de savants s'oubliant eux-mêmes pour sauver les hommes leurs frères, pour donner au monde un sort meilleur.

Elle m'a surtout montré d'un doigt impérieux le peuple de France courant sus à la Bastille où une lettre de cachet jetait des hommes dans les fers et la vermine.

Elle m'a donné avec le peu que je sais, le goût de la recherche, du travail fini, et élevé ma conscience à la conscience humaine.

En faisant tomber de mes yeux le voile ténébreux de l'ignorance elle m'a permis de humer le parfum d'un monde d'amour.

Elle m'a permis de voir, par delà mes misères, par delà mon taudis, par delà les montagnes d'injustices quotidiennes, un horizon de paix, une cité d'hommes frères ayant dompté les fléaux et l'égoïsme mortel.

Elle m'a dit, la France,
Elle m'a dit par ses savants, par ses martyrs, par ses héros, par son histoire, par son génie.

Elle m'a dit avec ferveur, me montrant les bastilles qui croulent sous son regard de feu:

Lutte pour que ce monde-là soit.

La France ne m'a donné ni le fusil, ni la poudre, ni les balles qui couchent à jamais des frères Noirs ou Blancs,

Mais en revanche, elle a éveillé en mon coeur, l'amour de l'humanité.

Août 1950

She showed me Pasteur and the band of scientists neglecting themselves to save their fellow men, to give the world a better fate.

She especially showed me with an imperious finger the people of France storming the Bastille where a "lettre de cachet" threw men into irons and vermin.

She gave me with the little I know the taste for research, for finished work, and raised my consciousness to human consciousness.

Lifting the dark veil of ignorance from my eyes she let me breathe the perfume of a world of love.

She let me see beyond my wretchedness, beyond my slum, beyond the mountains of daily injustice, a horizon of peace, a city of brotherly men having conquered scourges and mortal selfishness.

She told me, France
She told me through her scholars, her martyrs, her heroes, her history, her genius.

She told me with fervor, showing me the bastilles crumbling under her fiery glance:

Fight so that such a world can be.

France hasn't given me the rifle, nor the powder, nor the bullets which fell forever Black and White brothers,

But instead, she has kindled in my heart the love of humanity.

August 1950

Bernard Dadié

FRÈRE BLANC

Frère Blanc,
               dépassons le Jour,
                   les nuances,
                     La Nuit,
        La nuit des Noëls que je suis,

Regardons-nous de la montagne
Et bâtissons la cité sans frontière.

     Pavés

Sur la route du Temps

     Pions

Sur le damier du Sort,
L'hiver nous retrouve à pied d'oeuvre colmatant nos masures.

Frère Blanc,

Ton coeur n'est ni de marbre ni d'airain
       Rangeons nos masques.
Le coeur ne connaît pas de couleur
       que le rose de l'Amour
            et le bleu des Rêves.

Frère Blanc,
     Rangeons
          Prestige
             Empire

Bernard Dadié

WHITE BROTHER

White Brother,
        let's go beyond the Day,
         the shades,
           The Night,
    The Christmas nights that I am,

Let's look at one another from the mountain
And let's build the city without boundaries.

    Paving stones

On the road of Time

    Pawns

On Destiny's chess board,
Winter finds us on the site sealing up our hovels.

White Brother,

Your heart is not of marble nor of brass
    Let's put away our masks.
The heart knows no color
    save the rose of Love
        and the blue of Dreams.

White Brother,
    Let's put away
        Prestige
          Empire

Bernard Dadié

Ombres augustes
      grands chapitres
           de notre histoire.

    Nous sommes du siècle
    Ton coeur est de chair
       Je le sais
    Le mien aussi
      Tu le sais.

Frère Blanc,
       Tu es un homme
       Et moi aussi

        C'est tout dire.

           1958

LITANIE D'UN SUJET FRANÇAIS

De la force brutale,
      Délivrez-nous, Seigneur.
Des maîtres de guerre et des conquérants,
      Délivrez-nous, Seigneur.
Des agents secrets et des flics,
      Délivrez-nous, Seigneur.
De l'Europe libératrice de peuples dits opprimés,
      Délivrez-nous, Seigneur.
De la conquête européenne,
      Délivrez-nous, Seigneur.

Bernard Dadié

August shades
                great chapters
                                of our history

            We are of the century
            Your heart is of flesh
                I know it
            Mine too
                You know it.

White Brother,
                You are a man
                And I am too

                That says everything.

                1958

LITANY OF A FRENCH SUBJECT

From brute force,
            Deliver us, Lord.
From masters of war and conquerors,
            Deliver us, Lord.
From secret agents and cops,
            Deliver us, Lord.
From Europe the liberator of the so-called oppressed peoples,
            Deliver us, Lord.
From European conquest,
            Deliver us, Lord.

Des fonctionnaires zélés, ennemis du progrès,
  Délivrez-nous, Seigneur.
Des monopoles exclusifs et de la politique coloniale,
  Délivrez-nous, Seigneur.
Des experts en questions africaines,
  Délivrez-nous, Seigneur.
De l'hypocrisie du conquérant et de la cupidité de certains
  sujets,
  Délivrez-nous, Seigneur.
Apaisez les mânes de nos morts tombés au service du maître.
Rendez-nous nos joies, nos chants et nos espoirs.
Bannissez d'entre nous les convoitises et les expansions par
  lesquelles l'on asservit des peuples entiers . . . Amen!

From zealous bureaucrats, enemies of progress,
>   Deliver us, Lord.
From exclusive monopolies and colonial policy,
>   Deliver us, Lord.
From experts on African questions,
>   Deliver us, Lord.
From the hypocrisy of the conqueror and the cupidity of certain
>   subjects,
>   Deliver us, Lord.
Calm the shades of our dead fallen in the master's service.
Give us back our joys, our songs, and our hopes.
Banish from us the greed and the expansion through which
    entire peoples are enslaved . . . Amen!

Tchicaya U'Tam'si

TCHICAYA U'TAM'SI, POET OF THE CONGO

Born in 1931 in Congo-Brazzaville (the former French colony, as opposed to Congo-Kinshasa, the former Belgian colony), U'Tam'si came to France at the age of 15. He displayed a prodigious gift for poetry and published his first collection in 1955. In 1957 he returned to the Congo to work with his great hero, Lumumba, and the cause of independence. U'Tam'si edited the newspaper *Congo* in Leopoldville until Lumumba's arrest during the turmoil following Congolese independence from Belgium. Since then U'Tam'si has represented the Congo in the educational department of UNESCO, never ceasing to write rich poems. His use of displaced syntax, reminiscent of Césaire's, and of private and public symbols inspired by the Congolese oral tradition, makes his poems difficult to approach, but extremely rewarding. The following lines have been excerpted from *Epitome,* a collection that won the Grand Prix for poetry at the World Festival of Black Art held in Dakar in 1966. The main poem in the collection is a long epic about the turbulent struggle for Congolese independence; it resembles a "Passion" (or Crucifixion) poem and deals with a problem central to the poet's whole work, the Black-Christian confrontation. The poem included here comes after the epic and comments on the dilemma that Christianity, an imposed Western religion, poses for the native African.

Tchicaya U'Tam'si

LE CONTEMPTEUR (fragments)

À Catherine Bailly

Je bois à ta gloire mon dieu
Toi qui m'as fait si triste
Tu m'as donné un peuple qui n'est pas bouilleur de cru
Quel vin boirai-je à ton jubilate
En cette terre qui n'est terre à vigne
En ce désert tous les buissons sont des cactus
prendrai-je leurs fleurs de l'an
pour les flammes du buisson ardent de ton désir
Dis-moi en quelle Egypte mon peuple a ses fers aux pieds

Christ je me ris de ta tristesse
ô mon doux Christ
Epine pour épine
nous avons commune couronne d'épines
Je me convertirai puisque tu me tentes
Joseph vient à moi
Je tète déjà le sein de la vierge de ta mère
Je compte plus d'un judas sur mes doigts que toi
Mes yeux mentent à mon âme
où le monde est agneau ton agneau pascal — Christ
Je valserai au son de ta tristesse lente

. . . . .

Tu me tentes
et je jouis
Je me perds par cette musique de ton âme
ce ne sont que pourtant les truies qui chantent faux
Et moi je danse mort pour la tristesse lente

Tchicaya U'Tam'si

THE SCORNER (excerpts)

To Catherine Bailly

I drink to your glory my god
You who have made me so sad
You have given me a people that is no distiller
What wine shall I drink at your jubilee
In this land that is not for vineyards
In this desert all the bushes are cactus
shall I take their yearly blooms
for the flames of the burning bush of your desire
Tell me in what Egypt my people wear leg irons

Christ I laugh at your sadness
oh my sweet Christ
Thorn for thorn
we have in common a crown of thorns
I'll convert since you tempt me
Joseph comes to me
I suckle already at your virgin mother's breast
I count more than one judas on my fingers than you
My eyes lie to my soul
where the world is lamb your pascal lamb — Christ
I shall waltz to the sound of your slow sadness

· · · · ·

You tempt me
and I thrill
I lose myself in this music of your soul
and yet it's only the sows singing off-key
And I dance dead for the slow sadness

Tchicaya U'Tam'si

Les vices de ma peau sont les trois clous de fer
dans tes mains et tes pieds
Que tu es sale Christ d'être avec les bourgeois
Leur luxe est un veau d'or au cou de leurs bourgeoises

Tchicaya U'Tam'si

The vices of my skin are the three iron nails
in your hands and feet
How dirty you are Christ from being with the bourgeois
Their luxury is a golden calf around the neck of their women

Biafran men in military training during civil war in Nigeria

ÉDOUARD MAUNICK, POET OF MAURITIUS

Mauritius, the small island southeast of Madagascar, was uninhabited before its discovery by Portugal in about 1510. The French followed the Dutch in 1715 and were routed by the British in 1810. One hundred fifty thousand Black slaves were imported from East and West Africa in the eighteenth century to grow sugar, and with the abolition of slavery in the nineteenth century, laborers for the plantations were brought from the Indian subcontinent, China, and Madagascar. As a result, two-thirds of the population is mainly of Indian origin; the other third is mainly African or of mixed African and European descent. Our poet, Maunick (born in 1931), is of mixed blood but has chosen to be Black and writes in French, now a minority language on the mainly English-speaking island. He is considered one of the finest of the new generation of poets of Negritude. Like U'Tam'si's, his poetry is often difficult, even impenetrable. However, *Shoot Me,* a recent volume inspired by the civil war in Nigeria, has an immediacy that can be recognized in the excerpts included here. The poet mingles the themes of his private happiness, his island exile, and the vanity of writing, with the horror of Biafra, which finally silences him.

Édouard Maunick

FUSILLEZ-MOI (fragments)

pour ne rien inventer
pour ne rien trahir
mais pour assassiner
cet homme amant de sa parole
exilé dans ma vaine écriture!

au terme de moi et de la mer
l'alliance enfin avec le périr:
Biafra interdit au Biafra
Biafra acculé à la mer
une île qui ne saura pas quoi faire
de sa solitude et qui ferme les yeux...

Je me saborde au nom de tous les mots trop tristes
seul responsable de n'avoir pas de maison
aux murs tapissés d'algues et de tisanes douces
aux planches frottées de sable de bonne espérance
habitée par une femme à nommer nouvelle
et qui refuse mes raisons de naufrager...

Quel poème vais-je donc écrire alors que je n'ai pas
lu les journaux du matin et que ceux d'hier soir ne
donnaient pas encore le chiffre des morts:

 Pour un chiffre Biafra
 je vais te faire attendre
 dans le couloir comme un intrus
 et me rejeter dans ma petite vie
 avec une-grande-histoire-à-dire.

    • • • • •

Édouard Maunick

SHOOT ME (excerpts)

to invent nothing
to betray nothing
but to murder
this man lover of his words
exiled in my vain writing!

at the edge of myself and the sea
the alliance finally with perishing:
Biafra forbidden to Biafra
Biafra cornered by the sea
an island that doesn't know what to do
with its loneliness and closes its eyes . . .

I'm scuttled in the name of all the too sad words
alone responsible for not having a house
with walls papered in seaweed and sweet herbs
with floors scoured by the sand of good hope
where lives a woman called new
who refuses my reasons for shipwreck . . .

What poem then am I going to write when I haven't read
this morning's papers and last night's still didn't
give the number of dead:

>   For a number, Biafra
>   I'm going to make you wait
>   in the corridor like an intruder
>   and throw myself back into my petty life
>   with a-great-tale-to-tell

· · · · ·

Édouard Maunick

Jusqu'où vais-je aller ainsi, traînant ma seule mémoire alors que l'Histoire saigne abondamment et d'un sang plus juste que le mien? J'irai aux nouvelles dans quelques heures. C'est promis:

> Pour un temps Biafra
> je vais oublier ta mise à mort
> et jouer à l'inutile résurrection
> de ce qui me bâtit
> plus inutile que toi...

. . . . .

Et voilà que je parle de vivre par la vertu des morts. Quel chiffre avanceront-ils? Et comment le sauront-ils? Qui a trouvé le système de compter les morts de loin?

> Ibos Ibos j'ai froid pour vous
> et je parle de maison impossible
> dans une ville soûle de clarté
> ma légende me fait mal
> je crierai pour vous après...

. . . . .

Mais où vais-je puiser la force de me prétendre enfant du malheur quand tout le malheur de monde s'est donné rendez-vous au Nigeria?... Et qu'est-ce qu'un blanc qui m'insulte auprès d'un noir qui fusille un autre noir?...

> Biafra sans amour
> je ne saurais pas vous aimer
> elle doit venir elle est venue peut-être
> je vais la baptiser
> mais votre nom à vous sera rayé dynamité...

How long am I to go on like this, only my memory in tow, while History bleeds abundantly and with a more just blood than mine? I'll hear the news in a few hours. I promise:

> For a time Biafra
> I'm going to forget your execution
> and play at the useless resurrection
> of what built me
> more useless than you . . .

. . . . .

And here I am talking about living by the virtue of the dead. What number will they propose? And how will they know it? Who has found the system for counting the faraway dead?

> Ibos Ibos I'm cold for you
> and I talk of an impossible house
> in a city drunk with brightness
> my legend hurts me
> I will scream for you afterwards . . .

. . . . .

But where shall I draw the strength to claim I am misfortune's child when all the misfortune in the world has gathered in Nigeria? . . . And what is a white who insults me compared to a black who shoots another black? . . .

> Biafra without love
> I wouldn't know how to love you
> she must come she has come perhaps
> I'm going to baptize her
> but your very name will be crossed out dynamited . . .

Édouard Maunick

Maintenant que j'ai dit combien je pourrais vivre de m'être retrouvé. De n'être plus un étranger dans ma propre peau, de quel droit vais-je me retourner vers la mort de tout un peuple? Et pleurer?...

> Biafra Biafra tu recommences
> à me montrer du doigt
> Ibos Ibos vous me tutoyez
> et j'ai honte de répondre
> vivant... vivant... vivant!

· · · · ·

décalogue:
il y avait une fois une deux trois quatre cinq
cargaisons d'os et de chair qui avaient une âme
elles furent égarées dans les années soixante...
décalogue:
il y avait aussi six sept huit neuf dix
strates de cendres qui intriguèrent les chercheurs
elles furent identifiées au siècle des fusées lunaires...
décalogue:
sur les dix barreaux de nos mains lavées relavées
nous ne compterons plus jamais ni vingt ni cent
de ces Biafrais qui crurent en la Résurrection!...

Ce poème s'achève où commence ma vanité
les manèges de la mer tombent en ruines
dans ma peau dans ma tête dans ma voix
tournent tournent les manèges de la mort...

Édouard Maunick

Now that I've said how much I could live for having found myself. For no longer being a stranger in my own skin, what right have I to turn towards the death of a whole people? And weep?...

> Biafra, Biafra again you begin
> to point at me
> Ibos Ibos you call me "brother"
> and I'm ashamed to answer
> living ... living ... living!

. . . . .

decalogue:
once upon a time there were one two three four five
cargos of bones and flesh who had a soul
they were lost in the sixties
decalogue:
there were also six seven eight nine ten
layers of ashes that intrigued the researchers
they were identified as being from the century of moon rockets...
decalogue:
on the ten bars of our washed and rewashed hands
we will never again count twenty or one hundred
of those Biafrans who believed in the Resurrection!...

This poem finishes where my vanity begins
the merry-go-rounds of the sea[1] fall into ruins
in my skin in my head in my voice
turn turn the merry-go-rounds of death ...

---

[1]Title of an earlier collection of poetry for which Maunick was highly acclaimed.

Édouard Maunick

Il était une fois ma solitude
il était une fois mon exil
il était une fois mais laissez-moi
laissez-moi: on m'attend ailleurs qu'en moi . . .

Édouard Maunick

Once upon a time there was my loneliness
Once upon a time there was my exile
Once upon a time but leave me alone
leave me alone: they're waiting for me elsewhere than in
myself . . .

picture credits

1. *Léon Damas, Courtesy of Jeune Afrique.*
2. *Aimé Césaire, courtesy of the French Embassy Press and Information Division, 972 Fifth Ave., New York, N.Y.*
3. *Jacques Roumain, courtesy of Les Éditeurs Français Réunis.*
4. *Louis Armstrong, courtesy of the Columbia Record Company.*
5. *Léopold Senghor, courtesy of the Embassy of Senegal, Washington, D.C.*
6. *Bernard Dadié, courtesy of Jeune Afrique.*
7. *Tchicaya U'Tam'si, courtesy of Éditions Pierre Jean Oswald.*
8. *Biafran men in military training, UPI photo.*